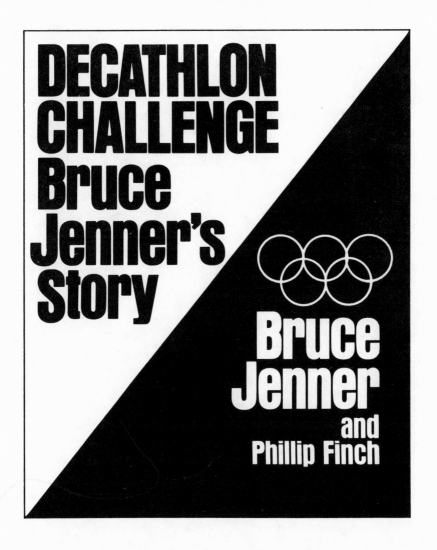

DECATHLON CHALLENGE
Bruce Jenner's Story

Bruce Jenner
and
Phillip Finch

PRENTICE-HALL, INC., Englewood Cliffs, New Jersey

*For Chrystie, Mom and Dad, Ron and L.D.
and for Francis D. Finch*

Decathlon Challenge: Bruce Jenner's Story
by Bruce Jenner and Phillip Finch
Copyright © 1977 by Bruce Jenner and Phillip Finch
All rights reserved. No part of this book may be
reproduced in any form or by any means, except
for the inclusion of brief quotations in a review,
without permission in writing from the publisher.
Printed in the United States of America
Prentice-Hall International, Inc., London
Prentice-Hall of Australia, Pty. Ltd., Sydney
Prentice-Hall of Canada, Ltd., Toronto
Prentice-Hall of India Private Ltd., New Delhi
Prentice-Hall of Japan, Inc., Tokyo
10 9 8 7 6 5 4 3 2

Library of Congress Cataloging in Publication Data

Jenner, Bruce,
    Decathlon challenge.
    1. Jenner, Bruce   2. Track and
field athletes—United States—Biography.
3. Decathlon.   I. Finch, Phillip.   II. Title.
GV697.J38A33   796.4'2'0924 [B]   77-4856
ISBN 0-13-197699-0

Preface

Bruce Jenner was twenty years old when he decided how he would spend the next few years of his life. He would run the decathlon. He was going to give up maybe six years of his life to running, jumping, and throwing. And he would do it not with a lucrative contract from a professional sports team, but strictly as an amateur. That alone is not such an uncommon decision. What sets Jenner apart is the single-minded way he attacked the decathlon. From that time on until the late evening of July 30, 1976, he measured both of his most trivial and most momentous decisions by a single standard: *Will it make me better in the decathlon?* He rejected anything that might stand in his way, that might blur the clarity of his life's purpose. This way he chose an apartment and assumed his temporary means of livelihood. This standard governed his diet, his sleeping habits, his daily routine. It was, alarmingly enough, surely one of his considerations when he decided to marry.

The vision narrowed even more after a couple of years. It was not enough to be a good decathlete. He was that already. Now he needed a world record and an Olympic gold medal, particularly the medal. And what had been mere dedication now turned into a fanaticism peculiar to geniuses, madmen, and great athletes. Jenner clearly was at least one of these.

Sport is too often a pointless, boring ritual. League standings change and are forgotten daily. Games pile on games, season upon season. New leagues blossom, and then die while others rise in their place. The stultifying mass of contests, scores, victories, and defeats defies appreciation. Notable deeds are obscured and diminished. Neither the joy of a championship nor the disgrace of a setback survives beyond the next game or the next season.

But it can be so much more. There are moments when sport becomes a mirror of humanity, reflecting human struggle, accomplishment, and defeat. It can be a setting for a morality play, for comedy or tragedy. It has this potential because it is a human activity, and because the drama is played out on a finite stage, with easily discernible dimensions. Winners and losers are rarely so well defined in the rest of life as they are in sport—by runs scored, distances jumped, time elapsed. The rules are clear, and so are the criteria for success or failure. No amount of dissembling can make a winner of a fighter who is prone on the canvas.

So sport can reduce life to its essentials, cut away all that is superfluous and confusing, permit us a glimpse now and then of the stuff of our existence. It has done that with Bruce Jenner. He could as easily have decided to become a great businessman, a great physician, a great salesman. But then his successes would have been less obvious, and any failures perhaps less biting. In his choice of the decathlon, his measure of greatness was simple: he would work as hard as possible and he would try to win the gold medal at Montreal. If he won the medal, then he would be a success. If he did any less, then he would have failed.

It was simple to understand. It could not have been more direct. And the decision clearly fixed the time, place, and character of his moment of reckoning: July 29 and 30, 1976, in the Olympic Stadium at Montreal. It could not be postponed or ignored. It hung before him, taunting and challenging him. And he was one of perhaps a half dozen athletes who could seriously hope to win that gold medal. Just as Jenner had given up years of his life to chase the gold, so had a Russian named Avilov and a German named Kratschmer and another American named Dixon. It was a heartbreak enterprise for all of them, a reckless crapshoot. In the special, carefully delineated way that sport provides, Montreal on July 29 and 30 became a vignette of human ambition.

This is the story of that high-stakes game and Bruce Jenner's part in it. It is about his striving and about what happened July 29 and 30 on the running track, the throwing circles, and the jumping pits at the Olympic Stadium. It is also about the decathlon itself, because that extraordinarily difficult contest attracts extraordinarily gifted and devoted athletes.

It happens to be a story about athletics because Bruce Jenner happens to be an athlete. But mostly it is a story about hoping and daring, winning and losing.

Phillip Finch

vi

I thought for a long time of doing a book about this period in my life, if only for myself. I knew that I was in the middle of something that was important. At least, it was important to me, and I wanted to have a record of it, something that I could have twenty or thirty years from now. Day to day, it's so easy to let time slip by and then it's gone and all the little details with it. I didn't want to lose that. Plus this record would give me a chance to examine myself and what I was doing, to stop for a while in the middle of it all and think, to remind myself of what I still had to do and how important it was for me. So this is it, as well as I can express it.

Bruce Jenner

Note: The first-person passages in Jenner's words are, for the great part, taken directly from taped conversations between Jenner and me that began the winter before the Olympics and continued for several weeks after Jenner's victory in Montreal. Much of his contribution to the book, therefore, was made without knowledge of the final outcome. Where pertinent to do so, such passages have been dated. In these passages, there are occasional contradictions. This is only natural, since Jenner's mood and outlook were not always constant. These inconsistencies have been retained in an effort to preserve the portrait of a man in the midst of the greatest struggle he may ever know.

I would like to thank L. D. Weldon, Frank Zarnowski, Dr. Leroy Perry, Sam Skinner, Jim Bainbridge, and Al Feuerbach for their time and help. Frank Zarnowski's *Decathlon Guide* and *Decathlon Book 1976*, by Zarnowski and Bert Nelson, proved to be invaluable reference sources for one confronted by the bewildering statistical and human complexity of the decathlon. And thanks to Fred Dickey.

P. F.

Contents

"A big brick wall . . ."

The sport is bigger than the man. Any man. Nobody ever shaped the decathlon to his own image, altering the basic character of the sport to fit his own talents. That is not such an absurd notion. It has happened elsewhere. Babe Ruth changed baseball from a punch-hitter's game to a slugger's game. Many track experts who saw Alberto Juantorena run the 800 meters in Montreal now believe that what once was considered a distance race must now be regarded as a sprint. No athlete had ever run the 800 quite the way Juantorena did. He altered the essential character of the race.

But nobody has ever done that to the decathlon. The sport is too rigid and too tough for that. Rather, it shapes and molds the athletes who would challenge it. It demands a special mind and a special kind of body, and that ideal has not changed for as long as anyone can remember. The men, then, come to resemble the sport.

Physically, the champions have changed little since Jim Thorpe won the first Olympic decathlon in 1912. The sport demands a compromise of physique: muscles that are strong and yet swift. Jim Thorpe was 5-feet-11, 181 pounds in 1912. Jenner is three inches taller, perhaps twenty pounds heavier, and nearly all the great decathletes fall within those boundaries. Bill Toomey was 6-1½, 190 when he won the gold medal. Nikolay Avilov was 6-3, 190 at Munich. There are exceptions: a young Russian named Rudolf Zigert who is 6-6, 235; a brilliant American decathlete of the 1960's named Russ Hodge, who was 6-2 and 225 when he competed; another American, Jeff Bennett, who was a world-class competitor at 5-8, 152. But the physical uniformity of the gold medal winners in the decathlon is no coincidence.

I think of the decathlon as a big, high, brick wall that nobody is ever going to be able to climb. It's cold and heartless. It has no mercy. It's awesome and scary. It will knock you down so fast. Nobody ever beats the decathlon. You might set a record and kick the hell out of it one day, but you know that it'll always be there, standing there, waiting for you to try again, telling you, "Okay, you son of a gun, try and get me this time." You've got to play by its rules. It's very regimented, right down the line. You make one slip, and it's got you. Just one mistake and it tells you, "To hell with you, this is all the points you're going to get."

That's especially true in a big meet like the Games or the Olympic Trials. If you run a race just a fraction too slow, or if you put the shot or throw the javelin just a little less than you know you can, then it will just kill you. It can come down to the last race, the 1500 meters, and you may run your guts out but still come up 15 or 20 points short. That's nothing. Nothing. The way the scoring tables are set up, you can pick up 15 or 20 points anywhere in the meet. That's a couple hundredths of a second in one place, a half an inch somewhere else. I could spend the rest of my life remembering all the times I could have picked up 15 or 20 points and didn't.

The decathlon has been called the most difficult of athletic events. Whether that is so is probably a matter of definition. It is not as painful or as debilitating as the marathon run—a

4

26-mile, 385-yard footrace that the best runners cover at a pace which most joggers couldn't maintain for a half mile. In comparison, the 1500-meter run that ends the decathlon is a carefree romp.

But probably no other sport asks so much of the athlete in so many ways as the decathlon during its two days of competition. The order of battle (100-meter sprint, long jump, shot put, high jump, and 400-meter run the first day; 110-meter high hurdles, discus, pole vault, javelin, and 1500 meters the second) encompasses the most technically difficult events in track and field. Every one of the ten demands a good measure of natural athletic ability.

And the demands are not merely varied. They are contradictory. Coaches and physiologists have many theories why this should be so. They can go on about how the height necessary for good throwing leverage is a disadvantage in running a sprint race, or the fact that fast-twitch muscle fibers are a poor substitute for the hard, stringy muscles to be found in any good distance runner's thighs and calves. But none of this is half as eloquent as the sight of a 250-pound discus-thrower trying to pole-vault, or a skinny 1500-meter runner heaving the shot. A decathlete does all that, and more. There are at least five distinct skills without which a decathlete is lost: sprinting, middle-distance running, weight-throwing, jumping, and what might be called coordination—important in such events as the pole vault or the javelin, which demand a combination of speed and power and a firm grasp of difficult technique.

It all begins the morning of the first day with the 100 meters, a pure and most comprehensible athletic event. It is a sprint over a distance slightly greater than the length of a football field, and it is over so quickly that most runners are not aware of having drawn a breath.

It's a scary event for a decathlete, because of the difference in points that a couple tenths of a second can make. If a guy beats you by two-tenths, he's up more than 50 points. The fact that it's the first event of all means that you bring with you all your tension and anxiety and pressure. And in less than ten seconds, all that is gone. When the race is over, I stop and take a deep breath. Literally.

Before I go into the blocks, I look down the lane. There are stripes marking the lanes and I look down the track to where those stripes converge like railroad tracks in the distance. I think about getting my body from here to there just as quickly and efficiently as I can. In the blocks, I concentrate on the sound of the gun. You don't get disqualified in the decathlon for your first two false starts, so it doesn't hurt to try to jump the gun the first time. You're crazy if you don't. I try to be a step out of the blocks the moment the gun goes off. Obviously, that's impossible. That would be a false start. But it takes a minimum of a tenth of a second to react to the sound and you try to eliminate that reaction time by anticipating the gun so that you're in the act of moving when the gun goes off.

I think of the 100 as two different races. There's the first 60 yards when you're gathering speed, accelerating, getting up to your maximum. If you're good and if you run the race well you may reach your maximum speed in 55 yards, or even 50. So much the better. The second part of the race is holding what you've got. Your stride lengthens out. It's like shifting gears, relaxing, and letting the speed that you've built up just carry you along to the finish. Then, 10 yards from the finish, there's a little drive to the tape. You try to lean because those few hundredths of a second can make a difference.

The long jump is another basic event. Anybody can identify with that, right? I make an 118-foot approach run. I can't tell you how many steps I take but I know that it's the same number each time. I use a tape to measure the distance from the takeoff board down the approach ramp. I mark the distance with a strip of adhesive tape and I hold my left foot on that line and take my first step with my right. I try to accelerate smoothly. That distance of 118 feet is shorter than most jumpers use. But I prefer it because I like the feeling that I'm gaining speed right up to the moment that I leave the ground. I concentrate on the takeoff board coming up. The last time my left foot touches the ramp, I really crunch that step, take it flat-footed. I keep the center of gravity of my body as low as I can. Then my right foot hits the board and drives my leg up into the air. My technique in the air is really poor. There's nothing you can do to save a bad jump, anyway. I try to get my legs out in front of me any way I can before I hit the ground.

The takeoff board is a white wooden slab about 4 inches wide across the end of the approach ramp. Beyond the board is a strip of smooth clay. If the runner's shoe touches the clay, the jump is ruled a foul. Decathletes jump three times, with the longest jump counted in the scoring.

Some of the ten events are stylish and beautiful. The shot put, by contrast, is as graceless and ponderous as the 16-pound implement that the athletes try to shove as far as possible out of the throwing circle. Of all the events, it demands the most strength, and the muscles that a shot-putter develops are antithetical to the speed necessary in the sprints and the jumps. The movements that Jenner describes are a choreographed explosion, but the culmination of all that effort, the weak and shallow flight of a cast-iron grapefruit, is vaguely disappointing and anticlimactic.

I relax in the back of the circle with the shot tucked almost next to my left ear, cradled in the palm of my left hand and with my back facing the throwing sector. You turn the body halfway around as you swing the front foot—the right foot, in my case, since I'm left-handed—ahead of your body, and you slide the other across the circle. The object is to keep your weight low and have as much of the mass of your body behind the shot as you possibly can. You don't throw. You push the shot, try to get drive from your legs, and then extend the throwing arm quickly with as much force behind it as you can sustain. The shot rests on the ridge at the base of the fingers. You flick your wrist at the last moment to give it that last bit of impetus.

The decathletes get three throws in shot put, discus, and javelin competition. Only the longest throw counts. Stepping or falling out of the throwing circle is a foul and the throw is disqualified.

In the high jump and in the pole vault there is no limit to the possible number of attempts. The athletes try to clear a bar set at a specific height, and the height is gradually raised during the competition. Three misses at any height disqualifies the jumper, and he is credited with the highest mark he successfully jumped. If he fails to clear a single jump, the athlete is credited with zero points. That happens.

There are two styles of high-jumping. The older one was called the "straddle" or "roll" because that's the sort of motion the body would make going over the bar. One leg led the rest of the body over the bar. That's the way I learned to high-jump first because that was the only style around until about 1967.

That was when a jumper named Dick Fosbury originated what's known as The Flop. It's a far more natural way of jumping a height. The head and shoulders are the first to clear the bar, and the rest of the body follows almost automatically. I started flopping in 1971 and I've been jumping that way ever since. I take an eleven-step approach that's in the form of the letter "J." My first six steps are straight but off to the left side of the bar. Then I cut sharply on my left foot and take five more steps in an arc toward the bar. I plant my right leg, draw my left knee up almost until it touches my chest, and everything goes up.

Arms, hands, legs. Your body takes a quarter-twist around so that the back is toward the bar. The only thing to concentrate on is getting the hips high, over the bar. Do that and it ought to be a good jump. As the hips drop over the bar, the legs come up. Then you're over, and you land on the shoulders or flat on your back.

The last event of the first day is the 400 meters. It is neither a classic sprint nor a distance race, but it demands both the speed of a sprinter and the endurance of a mile-runner. There are several obstacles, Jenner says, in the 400 meters. The most formidable is the phenomenon he calls "the bear."

The bear. Every runner knows about the bear. He's that invisible animal that waits for you about a hundred yards from the finish line. He jumps on your back and starts clawing and scratching and he seems so heavy that you want to stop running so that he'll get off and leave you alone. If you don't know the bear, then you've never run 400 meters.

It's the only physically tiring event of the first day, and the fact that it comes at the end of the day shows me that somebody had some foresight in planning the decathlon.

The only way to describe the technique is to say that you get your momentum going as soon as possible—you don't loaf out of the blocks—and then you try to maintain it to the tape. A whole lot easier to say than to do. Each runner starts in a different spot on the track, since the outside lanes are longer than the inside ones and you're not allowed to run out of your assigned lane. Depending on where you start, you could end up coming out of the starting blocks right in the middle of the first turn. That's your first big obstacle. Then there's the back stretch. I try to run nice and relaxed and get ready for the second turn. Anytime you change direction, you slow down. To compensate for that, I've always saved a little bit of energy for

9

running that last turn. I try to sprint a little harder to compensate for the turn. In the last 100 yards, well, you try not to let the bear get to you. You try not to slow down more than the next guy.

To me, the secret of a great decathlon comes at the end of the first day, after you've run the 400 meters. Whenever you have a hard, sustained output of energy like you've got in the 400 meters, your body builds up an excess of lactic acid. If the lactic acid stays in the muscles overnight, you've got cramps and sore muscles the next morning. So as soon as I've finished running the 400 meters, I jog at least a mile. That gives the blood a chance to carry away the acid. Then I do stretching exercises. I'm very conscientious about it and I've never had any problems the morning of the second day. At most, there are just a few kinks that work themselves out when I jog and warm up for the 110-meter high hurdles.

The hurdles race is an all-out sprint. The hurdles are three and a half feet high and there are ten of them in each lane, 10 meters apart. I've never been as good at the hurdles as I should be. The technique isn't all that complicated, but it seems as though some little thing is always going wrong.

The four events that remained were Jenner's strongest. Once he became a world-class decathlete, no one could stay with him through the finishing four. Among U.S. decathletes, only Rafer Johnson threw the 4-pound, 6-ounce, dish-shaped discus farther than Jenner on his best day.

Sometimes the only warm-up I take in the discus is a single standing throw, just to loosen up the arm. I discovered a couple of years ago that my first throw in warm-up was usually better than any other. So I began saving that one for the competition.

You start in the throwing circle with your back to the

sector and the arm extended straight out with the discus. You make a complete 360-degree turn and then another half turn just at the moment of release. It's very quick and explosive. The image I have in my mind is of a cat who is poised to pounce on a mouse, and then just flicks his paw out so fast to grab it. That's the release in the discus. That's what you shoot for.

The wind, says Jenner, can make a difference of as much as 15 feet, depending on velocity and especially on direction. For a left-handed thrower, the ideal wind is a breeze that blows toward the southeast if he is throwing north. This is called a "quartering wind." But the ideal wind for left-handers like Jenner is disastrous for right-handed throwers.

The pole vault was my first event in track and field, and it's probably my best in the decathlon. It pays a lot of points, and very few decathletes can vault as consistently high as I can. I use a 131-foot approach down the ramp, which is about average. When I'm two strides from the pit, I raise one end of the pole over my head and the other end drops into the planting box in the ground. I'm going full speed at this point if I'm doing it right, and the moment the pole plants in the box, it starts to bend and I start to lift off the ground. I swing my legs up and over my head so that when the pole starts to spring back, I'm completely inverted with my legs pointed straight up into the sky. Sometimes it seems as though the pole will catapult you right up into the clouds. When you get your full height, your legs go over the bar and your torso twists around so that you can throw the pole away. And that same motion is what puts your body over the bar. I usually concentrate so much that I'm not even aware of falling.

It's a tough event. That upside-down move, hanging from a bent pole, is the single toughest position to hit in track and field.

The second toughest is the next event, the javelin. The javelin is a spear, thin and with a cord grip wound around the middle. You don't throw the thing. You get a running start, plant your feet, and pull the javelin over your shoulder. You start the motion with your weight on the back foot and you follow through with the weight transferring forward. There's a foul line that you can't cross, but I give myself plenty of room. I throw better if I don't crowd the line.

Which brings you to the finale, the 1500 meters. I've won more decathlons with this event than with any other, but there's not much to say about it. There's no special technique. It's a matter of conditioning, guts, and desire. I think of it as three separate segments of 400 meters apiece and then a last section of 300 meters. Three 400-meter laps at 70 seconds each and the last 300 meters in 45 seconds gives a 4:15. That's a great time. But very few guys can do that. There were a lot of times I couldn't.

The decathlon typifies the Greek ideal of moderation, that the most worthy man is the one who is moderately good at many different facets of life. I don't have outstanding natural ability in any event, not compared to guys like Al Feuerbach with the shot, Mac Wilkins or John Powell with the discus. But through hard work and general ability, I've become a good athlete.

There are always guys with incredible ability in two or three different events who would seem to be perfect for the decathlon. Maybe they're great high-jumpers, good in the long jump, and you know that they must be good sprinters, too, just watching them run. That takes care of four or five of the ten events right there. But they never seem to get around to doing it, and the reason is work. Suppose a fellow is a really good, world-class sprinter. Why should he try the decathlon? A sprinter who's born with talent doesn't have to work that hard or train with that much dedication. He can win the medals and get the satisfaction *in his individual event. He has no reason to put up with the hassle of the decathlon. There's no way of avoiding the hours that go into winning a medal in the decathlon.*

First, you've got to be in good shape physically. Then you've got to be in good shape mentally, because so much of the decathlon is in the mind. Then you've got to learn the technique. There's a technique for throwing the javelin, another for putting the shot, another for running the hurdles, one for each of the ten events. In some of them, like the pole vault and the javelin and the jumping events, you're totally lost without good technique. All the ability and good conditioning in the world aren't worth a thing without it. A sprinter trains totally differently from the way a 1500-meter man trains. It's the same with a long jumper and a shot-putter, a javelin-thrower and a hurdler. They are diametrically opposed. But I have to be good at all of them. The only thing all those different athletes have in common is that they're all in good shape. So during the fall and winter, the off-season, I get in shape. I lift weights and I run, run, run, and by the time spring comes along, I've got a good physical base to work with.

It's an incredible athletic challenge; that's what attracted me to it in the first place. The whole idea is to take all ten events with all the different things you have to do and find some kind of balance in your body and mind.

Balance. The word recurs constantly in talking of the decathlon. The decathlete is a balanced man, not too quick or too big but, if he is lucky, quick enough and big enough for what he must accomplish.

By temperament and by physique, Jenner was an ideal decathlete. He admits that until he ran his first decathlon, "I was a mediocre athlete, compared to others. I had a lot of talent but there were a lot of people better than I was in everything I tried." But the decathlon more accurately reflected his potential than any single event ever could. He was

13

not mediocre. He was *balanced*. There were many things that he could do quite well. And he had an intuitive understanding of his body's workings that would later become invaluable.

The night after Jenner won the decathlon in the 1976 Olympic Trials at Eugene, Oregon, I talked with Dr. Leroy Perry, a chiropractor in the Los Angeles area whom many top U.S. track and field athletes revere for what they describe as near-miraculous treatments of their chronic muscular problems. He specializes in applied kinesiology—the study of muscles and their motions—adapting concepts of rehabilitation to sports. Though Jenner was not originally one of Dr. Perry's devotees, he did consult the man after listening to some of his friends talk so enthusiastically about the results of his treatments.

At Eugene, Dr. Perry spoke to me about athletes, about the decathlon, and about Jenner:

"There are a lot of variables that go into why one guy is a sprinter and another is a miler, why some are successful and others are not. You have to look at body type and muscular development. Part of it is coaching. There are dozens of examples of athletes who got stuck doing the wrong things, wrong for their own abilities. You see it all the time: a guy is just a mediocre quarter-miler but turns into a champion in the 100-yard dash. Then there's congenital ability and family background and psychological makeup. And you've got to know what your body can do. Maybe you've never high-jumped before, but you just have a feeling that you would be good at it.

"Bruce has the body for the decathlon. He's a good specimen of a mesomorph, not too skinny or too big. He's not overweight, yet his muscle development is outstanding. He's got speed, the fast-twitch muscles, yet he has stamina and power, too. He also has a unique mind, a unique psyche. He manages to stay pretty much aloof and relaxed through everything. That's the best thing you can have going for you in the decathlon, because as soon as you tighten up, you're through. He can psych himself down, instead of out.

"Today, between events, he was coming back to the rubdown table, relaxing and going through his own little self-analysis. You can watch his face and know what's going on. He's retracing what he's done, how much energy he's spent, then figuring out what he still has to do and how much he has left to do it with. It's as though he's got a little computer inside of himself, ticking away and telling him how much he'll be able to do and what he won't be able to do. Whether he's aware of the process or just does it automatically doesn't make any difference. I've seen him do it too many times to deny that it happens.

"As far as his body goes, he's got a unique response factor. I think Bruce is going to capitalize on any kind of workout he might do, whether it's swimming or weight lifting or running. He has a body that gets the maximum benefit from whatever he puts into it. He's had a few muscle balance problems, but he responds quicker to applied kinesiological techniques than the average athlete, even quicker than most world-class athletes. He has a one-of-a-kind body and psychological ability to relate to his body. He's interested in nutrition, follows a well-defined program. He had it pretty well worked out in his mind to begin with, before I ever talked to him.

"In fact, he develops himself to a plateau in everything he does. He's got to be at the top of what he does because he has left himself no alternative to the decathlon. He knows what he's doing. He's right on top of his life."

I asked Dr. Perry how his applied kinesiological therapy had affected Jenner's performance.

The only problem, he said, was a weakness in Jenner's abdominal muscles. With a program of 30-degree and 40-degree sit-ups, Dr. Perry said, "he strengthened exceedingly fast.

"What I've done for Bruce," he said, "has been very minor.

15

The results would be hardly discernible: a few centimeters in a shot put, maybe, or a couple of hundredths of a second in a sprint. A very minor tune-up. It's hard to better perfection."

The decathlete prizes his time. He hoards his hours and parcels them out sparingly. The ten events seem to squall for attention like hungry infants. So he tosses them scraps and chunks of his time. One portion he grudgingly sets aside for eating, sleeping, and a minimum of daily routine. An appalling amount is also reserved for rest—not because he is lazy, but because the hardest training is useless if the body is too weary to absorb the effect. That leaves so very little time for running and vaulting and throwing. The decathlete becomes a diplomat, conceding time to a weakness in his pole vault, perhaps stealing a few hours from his long jump to fatten up the discus. He hammers out a bargain between his body and the relentless passing of the days. And then the bargain is tested when he goes against the tables.

This is the skeletal structure of the decathlon. Without the tables, the event has no form or definition. Decathletes talk about the tables the way Moslems talk of the Koran and the way U.S. Supreme Court justices speak of the Constitution. The tables are an arbitrary grading of performances in each of the ten decathlon events, broken down into tenths or hundredths of seconds, by feet and by fractions of inches. As an athlete runs faster, jumps higher, throws farther, the tables concede him more points. If the balance is off, if that delicate personal bargain is weak, then the tables will show the weakness. The tables have been revised four times since 1912 to reflect advances in technique, performance, and equipment. The present tables favor athletes who are strong in the pole vault and the sprinting events, since even a relatively weak performance in those events (when compared to the existing world records) pays relatively high points. But those comparisons are meaningless. The tables are supreme, and the athlete must bend to conform with them. That is the rule of

16

the game, and those who find it unpalatable belong else-where. Experienced decathletes spend remarkably little time griping about inequities in the system.

There's a lot of satisfaction in being able to compare myself with every guy who ever ran the decathlon. That's because of the tables. Every man who ever ran the decathlon ran against the tables, and there's no way of cheating them.

In football, there's no set standard for your perform-ance. You know that a guy is a good running back if he gains a lot of yards and is hard to tackle. But you don't know how good he really is, compared to another good running back. Even by comparing the number of yards each gains, you've only got half the story. How can you measure which one is the better blocker? Which one is the better pass receiver? People are going to be arguing forever who was a better back, O. J. Simpson or Jimmy Brown. But it's futile to argue because there's no absolute test of their abilities. If you want to compare me with Avilov or Toomey or Kurt Bendlin or anybody else who ran against the current tables, well, it's a lot easier to draw some conclusions.

It is one of the ironies of the sport that a decathlete, if he has truly found that elusive balance between contradictions, can win a decathlon without winning a single event. He is com-peting as much against the tables and himself as he is against the other athletes.

An immensely talented Formosan athlete, C. K. Yang, won seven of the ten events in the 1964 Olympic decathlon. Rafer Johnson was first in only one, the shot put. But Johnson stayed close enough to Yang in each of the others—and outdistanced him so much in the discus, the shot, and the javelin—that he led Yang by 65 points going into the last event, the 1500 meters. Yang was superior in the event, while Johnson tended to dismiss it. But in growing darkness, with the gold medal at stake, Johnson went striding out with Yang. Johnson stayed close, finished just a second behind Yang, and lost just 7 points of his lead. Johnson won the gold medal, for he had found the balance.

Jenner, perhaps, found it more surely and more often than anyone since an American, Glenn Morris, won the 1936 gold medal with a world-record 7,900 points. Just as Morris did those two days in Berlin, and as Thorpe had done in 1912, Jenner by 1975 was running decathlons that were without apparent weakness. He was not truly outstanding in any one event. But neither did he lose a great number of points in any one. He was strong and consistent in every one, generally finishing in the top three of every event, even in international meets.

Avilov was a relatively weak pole-vaulter whose personal best was under 15 feet. Fred Dixon was a superlative sprinter but was weak in the pole vault (13 feet) and the 1500. Toomey only once vaulted as high as 14 feet and ran only 4:39.4 in the 1500 the day he set his world record of 8,417 points. Johnson's time of 4:49.7 in winning the gold in 1960 was a full nine seconds slower than even Thorpe had run the race in 1912, and 37 seconds slower than Jenner at Montreal.

Jenner was a reliable 15-foot vaulter who consistently ran under 4:20 in the 1500. Dixon might run the sprints faster, Avilov might jump higher and longer, but never fast enough or far enough to make up for their deficiencies when compared to Jenner.

Jenner's strength in the second-day events helped him to buck another trend. He is one of the few decathletes consistently to score more points the second day of competition than the first. He rarely led a decathlon on the evening of the first day. He usually dropped some points on the morning of the second day to the more accomplished runners in the 110-meter hurdles. But from that time on, he was at his best while the others struggled.

It all started at the U.S. Trials in 1972, when I came from eleventh place at the end of the first day to finish third and win a spot on the U.S. team. Next, at Munich, I was twenty-third after the first day and ended up tenth. After a while, everybody got to know it: Jenner is strong the second day. I think it's a great position to be in. It tends to take away the advantage of leading. They can be 200 points ahead after the 400 meters and still not know whether that's enough, whether I'm really going to put together a great second day and just run away from them.

It'll be the same at Montreal. They'll know I'm back there. They'll know that I'm going to go over 15 feet in the pole vault and run a 4:10 in the 1500 if I have to. It's got to make them nervous.

That threat was obvious because of another statistical dimension: a high-water mark for each athlete in each event. The athletes call it a "p.r.," for "personal record." Many decathletes, including Jenner, take the concept ever further. Jenner can recite a string of his p.r.'s that includes weight-lifting exercises and running workouts. The p.r. is a measure of progress and of potential. The ideal is to approach or exceed one's p.r. in each event, in each decathlon. Avilov met or set seven personal records while winning the gold medal and setting a world record at Munich in 1972. It was the decathlon of a lifetime and, significantly, he never came close to that total again. Russ Hodge would have scored almost 9,000 points if he had ever been able to come close to each of his p.r.'s in a single decathlon. But the balance eluded him.

Physically, the decathlon is not that tough. I work harder some days in training than I do in a day of competition. I run farther, I do more. And I do it in less time. But the competition is much more exhausting because of the mental

19

stress. *Being able to cope with that is what separates the good decathletes from the rest.*

Your mind can get you through a tough spot even when your body isn't up to it. In the 1974 AAU National meet, I wanted to knock Bill Toomey's meet record out of the books. I was pretty close to doing it after I vaulted a p.r., 15-9. But I took so many jumps to get there that I exhausted myself. My legs were shaking; I was so worn out that I didn't want to do anything but lie there. But my mind was still strong when we went out to run the 1500. I had to do a 4:15 to beat the record. I went out at a decent pace, but on the last lap I knew I had to push myself. My legs started to move, I started to pull away. I was doing it with my mind, you see, because my legs were finished. Even in the last 10 yards I was telling myself, "Okay, you haven't come all this far to let it get away from you," and I started to sprint. I leaned at the tape just like a sprinter. I ran 4:13.6, which was a p.r. for me at the time.

The mind—at least, my mind—works so strangely. Even a good performance can hurt you if you don't keep yourself under control. I can remember quite a few times getting so high over a good mark in the previous event that I got out of control in the next one. If I put the shot really well, I've got to force myself to take it easy, get that out of my mind and concentrate on what I've got to do next in the high jump. I try to do it step by step, ignoring the pressure the best I can, just trying to get maximum points out of each event. It may sound silly, but all that mental effort saps your strength. Physically, you haven't done that much. Toward the end of the second day, if you've spent a long time vaulting, maybe your body should feel a little physical fatigue. But if you look around the track before the start of the 1500, you'd think everybody out there had just finished running the marathon. Half of the athletes are lying around, breathing hard, looking as though they don't have the energy to get up off the ground and run another race.

That's because you concentrate so much. Too much, sometimes. And then your mind can go blank. I've had it happen to me more than once. I'll be standing in the middle of the shot put ring, and all of a sudden I think to myself, hey, what am I doing here? I've got this big iron ball in my hand and I don't have any idea what I'm supposed to be doing with it. It's true. I don't know any of the motions, I don't know what I'm doing. It's an awful feeling, let me tell you. There's only one thing to do then. You step out of the circle just as if nothing's happened, you take a deep breath and you back up about three paces in your mind. A horrible feeling.

Perhaps no other athletic event taxes the mind as completely as the decathlon. Surely none imposes such stress for so long a time. The time of actual competition is relatively short, probably less than a half hour. But there is a minimum of 30 minutes' rest between events, and large fields of competitors mean long waits between attempts in the high jump and the pole vault. From the first heat of the 100 meters on the morning of the first day to the last heat of the 1500 the evening of the second, the competitors are on the track at least fifteen hours. It is not an ideal spectator sport.

But that pace is precisely why the competition is so taxing. There is time, too much time, for an athlete to dwell on the event that he has put behind him and the events to come. He can ponder the scores, replay in his mind his successes and failures so far. There is much working time for doubt and fear. As the athlete sits on the grass waiting his turn, irritations can be magnified, apprehensions can swell, doubt can gnaw away at confidence. To keep the mind on the job at hand and yet free from doubt is a formidable mental task. Jenner did it well.

When you get more than a dozen entries, it starts to get awfully tiresome. In the long jump you're waiting twenty minutes, maybe, between tries. That means you get warmed up, you jump, then you sit around and wait so long that you've got to warm up all over again before you make your second jump. It hurts the performance. It has to. It also means that you've got plenty of time to psych yourself right out of a good jump.

But because of all the time that decathletes spend together on the track, they get to know each other a lot better than athletes in most other sports. You learn something about each guy, what his strengths and weaknesses are, and you've got a chance to observe him in so many different situations. You get a feeling for one another. I've had fans tell me that they get the same feeling just from sitting in the stands. The athletes are out there so long that the spectator starts to get involved with them. The guy in the stands feels that he knows you. He gets very emotionally involved. He feels as though he's been through something right along with those guys down there on the field. Which he has, in a way.

The feeling is one of having taken part in a grand ordeal. The athletes seem to grow in stature. Their feats become more and more improbable. From the tedium of the long hours grows a real respect. One who was suitably impressed was King Gustav of Sweden. He told Thorpe after presenting him with his gold medal in 1912, "You are the greatest athlete in the world." ("Thanks, King," Thorpe is supposed to have answered.) The king's appraisal has been generally accepted ever since.

Am I the world's greatest athlete? I am, if anybody is. That takes in such a great area. What I am, really, is the world's greatest decathlete. If you want to use the decathlon as a test of total athletic ability, then I guess I'm the world's greatest athlete. It's as good a test as any. But that sure doesn't help me when I stand up at a tee and try to hit a golf ball. Then I'm just another guy who can't hit straight. And it doesn't help me when I'm trying to play tennis, either. I think I'd have been good at those sports if I'd concentrated on them the way I concentrated on the decathlon, but I'm not saying that I'd have been the world's greatest, either.

The question seems not to concern him. He is now one of an impressive string of decathlon champions. That is what he always wanted, and that is more than enough for him. Thorpe, Mathias, Johnson, Jenner. Yes, he would be pleased to have his name slide in there. They were great athletes. Moreover, they are *remembered* as great athletes, as few track and field performers have been. And they are remembered, somehow, as great men, maybe because we perceive in them a spirit that is universally admired. Something like the "character" that high school football and 20-mile hikes with full knapsacks are supposed to instill in young men. However it is defined, that spirit is the one essential for running the decathlon. Without it, a man might as well try competing with his legs in shackles or with one arm strapped behind his back.

Thorpe, Mathias, and Johnson are touchstones of our athletic legend. Yet there are other champions—Osborn, Bausch, Campbell, Morris—who have been forgotten except as footnotes in athletic history. Harold Osborn won Olympic gold both in the decathlon and the high jump in 1924 at Paris. James Bausch set a world record while winning the gold in Los Angeles in 1932. Milt Campbell won a silver medal when he placed second to Mathias in 1952, then set an Olympic record and beat Johnson by 350 points to win the gold medal in Melbourne in 1956. Morris set a world record and led an American sweep of the decathlon in the 1936 Games at Berlin. And while Bill Toomey is remembered for his 1968 gold, he has not yet achieved that somehow larger than life status which seemed to go to Thorpe, Mathias, and Johnson by divine right.

And yet they were all great men. Jenner never knew most of them, but he is sure of that much. When they laced up their spiked shoes and went out to run and jump and throw, they had to be great men. Because the decathlon, that great indomitable brick wall which forever exceeds men's talents and ambitions, simply would not have tolerated them any other way.

"It looked like the end"

It was, by most standards, an ordinary American childhood. His father, Bill Jenner, was a tree surgeon in Westchester County, New York. His mother cared for the family home and for the two boys and two girls. They were neither rich nor poor. As for portent of athletic greatness in the older boy, the one named Bruce, these things can be pretty tenuous. It may or may not be important that his childhood nickname was "Bruiser." His mother, Esther, remembers that he was "a muscular little fellow when he was just a tot, just a year and a half, two years old." She says:

"He had a big chest and big wide shoulders. We called him 'Bruiser.' That's how I'll always remember him. He was such an active child. Not hyper, but always moving, always getting into things. I could never get him slowed down enough to look both ways before he crossed the street. When he wanted to cross, he went. We put a fence around the yard but that didn't keep him in. Finally we put him in a harness, put a stake in the middle of the yard, and tied a clothesline from the stake to the harness. And he didn't like that a bit. He's always been athletic, you know, and we encouraged it. But it was never anything that serious until one winter when he came home from college and started talking about the decathlon. From then on, that was all he talked about."

It was a remarkably unremarkable upbringing that probably has been duplicated many million times and it included a solemn reverence for sports. His father had competed in four events at the U.S. Army Olympics at Nuremberg in 1945, winning a silver medal in the 100-yard dash. His grandfather had run the Boston Marathon for fifteen years. So it was considered altogether fitting and proper for Bruce to play basketball for the school team in the sixth grade. About that time, Bill Jenner decided that the family needed a recreation in common, something they could do together. He considered quarter-midget race cars, the kind powered by lawn mower engines, but the women may have balked at the idea of changing pistons and spark plugs. But water-skiing, that was something else. The Jenners bought skis and a towboat and even a home on the Housatonic River in Connecticut. No half measures. And Bruce just happened to win the Eastern water-skiing championship three different times, once in the junior age group and twice as a senior.

When I was in junior high school, I had trouble with my right knee, something called Osgood-Schlatter disease. It's pretty common among growing kids, when the tendons don't grow as fast as the rest of the leg. But before the knee got bad, in seventh grade, I was on the school wrestling team. I lost my first seven matches in a row. I got pinned every time. I can still remember that feeling, looking up at the ceiling while the other guy was beating me. But then I won the next four in a row and I got to the county championship seeded first in my class, 106 pounds. I was a real terror. I got a bye in the first round because I was top seed, pinned the next guy, and that was how I got into the finals. I got beat by a point in the finals. That was quite funny because at one point we both had bloody noses, the other kid and I, and they had to stop the match for a few minutes

28

while we lay there on the mat with our heads tilted back so the bleeding would stop. I got beat by a single point. Then my knees started to bother me and the school wouldn't let me compete, so I started swimming and diving for the YMCA swim team. Actually, I was more of a diver. I only swam when they needed a fourth guy for a relay.

By my freshman year at high school, the knee was in good shape again so I played basketball and I ran track. I pole-vaulted on the track team. My first attempt at my first meet was at 8 feet, 6 inches. I was way over it, but I came straight down on the crossbar. My face hit the crossbar, and it tore my lip up and I fell down on the sand pit. I was lying there with my face bleeding, hurting all over, thinking, well, this is some sport! So this is track and field.

That was around the time I won the Eastern regionals in the water-skiing, jumping, and slalom. In 1966 I went to the national championships in Miami and did just terribly. I'd made 27 buoys to win the slalom at the regionals. Now I had gotten to the big time, all my family and friends there watching, and I got out of shape on the first buoy and fell on the second. I just lay there under water and I didn't want to come up. What's worse, to go to Miami I missed the first three days of football practice, which was a definite no-no.

I was a pretty good football player, playing outside linebacker. My junior year at Tarrytown High, we had a great team. We were undefeated going into the last game of the season. So was Ossining, which was the neighboring high school and our big rival. The two teams had been ranked 1-2 in the state for most of the season. That fall my parents had moved to the new home in Connecticut, but I stayed in Tarrytown and lived with a friend of mine, John Walton, long enough to finish the football season. There was so much traffic, so many people trying to get into this little high school stadium for the last game, that we had to climb off the bus and walk the last couple of blocks to the field. When we got there, it seemed like the field at Yankee Stadium for a Giants' game. I wound up making the front page of The New York Times the next day, a picture of me picking up a kickoff and getting tackled after I ran about ten yards. I got hit so hard that I fumbled and had to recover my own fumble. We got behind six-zip and didn't score for the first three quarters. We finally scored a touchdown with about three minutes left and I was supposed to catch a pass for the extra point that was going to win it, a special play that the coach had cooked up. I've never been so scared. Here are all these people yelling and screaming and I'm the one who's supposed to catch the ball. I walked out on the field thinking, "They're going to throw the ball to ME." I got clobbered coming off the line, the pass went over my head, and I felt really bad. But we scored another touchdown anyway, just as the gun went off. A running back carried the ball, got hit, and fell into the end zone. It's one of the biggest thrills I've ever had in sports. It meant so much at the time.

Jenner told me this story just a few days after he had won the gold medal at Montreal. But it was not some wistful reminiscence. He had been slouching in a chair in his living room, but as he told the story, he straightened his back and leaned forward. His face was alive and his voice became louder, taking on shades of emotion. It could have been a malt shop in Tarrytown the day after the big game, and he could have been recounting his exploits to a group of classmates.

There is another part to the story. When Ossining scored its touchdown, Jenner was playing defense. A receiver broke open and Jenner left his position to cover the man. But he was late, the man caught a touchdown pass and Jenner was caught looking silly.

"There was a live radio broadcast," Jenner said, "and the announcer said I was the guy who got beat for the touchdown. And most of the people in the stands thought I was to blame, too. It wasn't fair. Just because I was hustling. He wasn't even my man," he said.

His intensity—this was, after all, a ten-year-old high school football game, and not exactly the apex of his athletic career—surprised me.

"You still remember that, don't you?" I said.

"Damn right," he said. *"He wasn't my man."*

Two days after that game, I was back living with my parents and going to school in Connecticut, Newtown High. Things were a lot different there. Tarrytown was a big school, athletically oriented. But Newtown was so much smaller. I was the big jock on campus. I was Most Valuable Player in just about every sport I played, and I played all over. They used me as a running back and as an end, and I even played quarterback once in a while when we ran a shotgun formation. I played basketball and I ran track, too. I was state champion my senior year in the high jump and pole vault. That sounds really impressive, I guess. I won the high jump at just 6-2¼. I beat Ron Evans, who is now a good decathlete. And I pole-vaulted only 12-9. Those marks wouldn't even qualify me for the high school state finals here in California, but Connecticut isn't exactly what you would call a hotbed of track. I also finished third in the state meet in the triple jump, and I placed third or fourth as a team all by myself.

During all this time, he had never considered the decathlon something he might do. In fact, he never considered the decathlon at all, not even after a someone from the same county, Bill Toomey, won the gold medal at Mexico City in 1968.

Jenner was a tall, skinny kid then, probably 30 pounds away from the well-proportioned mesomorph who rippled across the TV screen from Montreal. He was a little afraid of girls. Mostly, he was just like the kid from down the street with whom you or your brother or your son played ball in the afternoon. Oh, he ran a little faster than most of the other kids and jumped a little better and generally seemed to have an easier time with the sweaty games than anybody else in the neighborhood. But that didn't make him any different. He was the Jenner kid, the kind of boy your parents used to hope you'd invite to your parties because he was so polite and quiet.

After my senior year at Newtown, I went to work with my dad, just as I'd done every one of the last few summers. But this time we talked about my going into business with him as a partner. I wasn't too sure I wanted to get into that so fast, but I didn't know about college, either. I wasn't a terrific student, never got into books all that much. And I didn't get a single offer for an athletic scholarship my senior year. This was about the time everybody was getting drafted into the army, too, so I had an idea the government might be making up my mind for me. It was just three or four days before school started in fall that Graceland got in touch with me. L. D. Weldon, the track coach, happened to know a high school coach in Connecticut. I got a call from L. D. and he asked me if I'd ever played quarterback. The truth was that I hadn't been much of a quarterback. Then he said, "Well, you run track, too, don't you?" I said I did. That was all he wanted to hear. He told me to pack my bags and get out to Iowa. He said that if I played two sports, I'd get the maximum athletic scholarship—$500 a year. This still wasn't a heck of a lot, since the tuition and expenses came to around $2,500 a year. But I had in the back of my mind that I wanted to get away from home for a while, and Lamoni, Iowa, seemed pretty far away. So I went to the bank that day to get a loan and took off the next morning for Graceland.

The football team needed a quarterback, and one of the coaches had asked Weldon's help in finding one, since he had just returned from a recruiting trip to the East. Weldon had heard about a kid named Jenner who sometimes played quarterback on the varsity team. But that wasn't all he heard about Jenner.

Weldon remembers: "One of the high school coaches that I knew told me this kid also ran track. He said the kid could high-jump 6–2, pole-vault about 13 feet, do the triple jump, and had even thrown the javelin 180 feet. We got some money out of the football program for him, but I had him figured for the decathlon all along. I knew that he must be able to jump, and that he had a good throwing arm if he could throw the javelin that well. Those two things, jumping and throwing, are the two most important abilities for the decathlon. Speed is important, too, but there are ways of getting around that. As a matter of fact, his speed wasn't very good at all."

Though Jenner didn't need much selling, Weldon was on the telephone in an hour with his pitch. He told the kid that Lamoni was a nice, quiet town of about 2,500 in the south-central part of Iowa, about five miles north of the Missouri line and about 80 due south on good roads from Des Moines. He said that the school enrolled 1,400 students every year, that it was run by the Reorganized Church of the Latter Day Saints (the ones who didn't go to Utah), and that it had a beautiful 38,000-square-foot field house with a 220-yard indoor running track. That sounded good enough to get L. D. Weldon's newest decathlon prospect on a plane to Des Moines.

But first there was football. Jenner still figured that he had come to Graceland to be a quarterback.

The first day of practice, I looked like a total jerk from the time I called my first play. Face it, I just wasn't a quarterback. We had a little scrimmage and the first pass I threw got intercepted by a defensive back. He went scooting down the sideline with the ball. I was the last guy with a chance to stop him, but I had a terrific shot at him from his

*blind side. He never saw me coming. Wham, I just about
took the poor guy's head off. His helmet went flying and he
landed about ten feet out of bounds. The defensive coach
came running over to me yelling, "Boy, you're no quarterback. You're going to play defense." And right there, he
made me change my jersey and I started playing defensive
back. About a month and a half later I was trying to block a
punt in a game. We had a play set up, with two guys on the
line supposed to crossblock and open up a hole. That part
worked. I went right through. There was a single blocker,
just in front of the kicker, and he hit my knee just as I was
springing up to block the punt. The knee was hyperex-
tended and I was out for the year.*

It was his right knee, and X-rays showed both ligament and
cartilage damage.

*I had surgery the day after New Year's, 1969, in Danbury,
Connecticut. As I was going out from the anaesthetic, I
looked up at the surgeon and said, "Doc, do a good job,
'cause I need this knee." I was lucky. The cartilage wasn't
so badly torn that they couldn't repair it. I've still got a
piece of metal in there, a staple.*

*He did a good job. About seven weeks later I started
working on it. It was so tight, it was like a big ball of
cement. But L. D. got hold of me and went to work on it.*

Weldon said: "I had him doing exercises at least once a day,
usually twice. I made him bend it when it hurt. I made him
yell a little bit. We did hot-and-cold treatments and that
loosened it up even more."

Within two weeks, the knee could bend 45 degrees. By the
end of the year it was as strong and as flexible as it had ever
been. Jenner never played football again. He did play basketball on the varsity team the next season ("He wasn't a very
good basketball player," Weldon says) and the knee had

recovered enough by the spring of his freshman year for him to throw the javelin 180 feet. Weldon had casually mentioned during Jenner's convalescence that he might try running a decathlon sometime during the next track season. By some conspiracy, Jenner's roommate that freshman year was not a football player, but a decathlete named Mike Mattox.

Jenner was still a competitive water-skier. Weldon thought it dangerous, and urged him to give up the sport. But that was asking a lot. Jenner was a very good water-skier, and he had never run a decathlon. He resolved the quandary in a fashion that seems totally out of character with the logical, calculated way he has run his life since 1972.

After my freshman year at Graceland I had pretty much decided that I wasn't going back to school. When my knee had gotten hurt, it looked like the end of my athletic career. L. D. talked about the decathlon, but I don't think I'd ever seen one at that time. It was something for me to think about, but I couldn't get too excited about it. I had a friend who had gone to Florida and gotten a job with a water-skiing show. He told me to come down and join him because there was a job for me, too. It sounded awfully good. I'd be making decent money, there was lots of sunshine and pretty girls, and I'd be doing something I had always enjoyed and had always been good at. It was the middle of the summer when I talked to this guy; I happened to be visiting another friend in Virginia. My mother wanted me to come back to Connecticut and go back to Graceland in the fall. My friend was talking up this job as a water-skier. The only drawback to that was that I would become a professional athlete, which would have been the end of my amateur athletic career. It really hadn't been much of a career so far, anyway.

I didn't know what I ought to do. I kept thinking about it. I threw my bags in the car and drove out to the Interstate Highway. I was torn. The distance from Virginia to Con-

necticut was about the same as from Virginia to Florida. Even that couldn't help me make up my mind. I was in the right-hand lane when I got to the Interstate. You had to turn right to go north—up to Connecticut—and left to go south, to Florida. I still hadn't made up my mind, when a woman pulled her car up beside me in the left lane. That meant I'd have had to slow down and pull in behind her if I wanted to turn left and go south. That was too much trouble, so it made up my mind for me. I turned right and headed north, back home. I went to Graceland that fall, ran track, and got into the decathlon.

It's awesome to me to think about how different my life might be if that left lane had been open. I'd never have met my wife at Graceland, never would have been an athlete. I look back on my life and I can see a thousand times, just the times I am aware of, where I had a choice to make or where things could have gone one way or the other. Everything worked out the right way to get me where I am. But it makes me think: how many other guys out there took the wrong turn? There are a lot of people out there who could be here instead of me. That's the most awesome part of all.

"I knew I had
found something"

*The first decathlon I ever saw was the first one I ever ran.
It was the Drake Relays, the spring of 1970. I'd heard of the
event, but never had any idea of trying it, until after I was
laid up my freshman year. L. D. mentioned it, and my
roommate and I used to talk about it quite a bit. So when I
went back for my sophomore year, I figured I would give it
a try in the spring. I'd been studying the tables, estimating
how I could do in each event. I added up all my points and
it came to about 7,000. This was kind of silly, since I had
never even tried some of the events.*

*I played basketball that year and I had only a month to
train for the decathlon after the basketball season was
over. I started working as hard as I could. I threw the shot
a little bit, and one week before the meet I ran my first
hurdles race, at the Dickinson Relays at the University of
Northern Iowa. In the hurdles you're supposed to take
three strides between each hurdle. That's the way it has to
be done. But you need speed and momentum to keep that
up. At the Dickinson Relays I three-stepped the first four
hurdles but then I lost my speed and I five-stepped all the
rest. I looked awful. I ran 19.3 and I thought I was in
trouble with my first decathlon coming up next week.*

This was to be the Drake Relays in Des Moines, a major college meet every spring. In the last several years the meet organizers have limited the entries to the fifteen high-scorers. But in 1970 that limit was not in effect and 32 entries were accepted, Jenner's included.

It was so strange. I never used to get too worked up about basketball or football games. I never missed any sleep over them, anyway. But I couldn't sleep the night before that first decathlon, knowing what was ahead of me.

Jenner remembers the day as cool and bright, good running weather. He ran his heat of the 100 meters in 11.2 seconds. Jeff Bennett, then developing into one of the country's best decathletes, won the heat in 10.5 seconds.

I'd never long-jumped before. But I was pumped, really high, since I'd run the 100 faster than I had expected. My first jump, I went 21 feet, 5 inches. That was way over what I'd figured. The second jump, I did 22-4 and just barely fouled. The third jump I fouled again, but cleared more than 23 feet. Even today, I have a hard time jumping that far. I was shocked that I did so well. I was totally fresh, didn't have a single idea of what I was doing, and maybe that helped. I just ran like mad down the runway and jumped.

His three throws in the shot put were all in the 38-foot range. Then, in the high jump, he cleared 6-3¾ before finally fouling out. Though he later switched to the Fosbury Flop method of jumping—head and shoulders first over the bar—his technique in 1970 was still the style called the "straddle." That height of 6-3¾ was an inch higher than his previous best. It was the highest he ever jumped until he switched to the Flop.

40

*I don't know how to explain it, except that I was so excited.
I was doing things that I never imagined. But I got cooled
off a little bit when we went to run the 400. I'd never run
the quarter before. I killed myself running 53.3 seconds. I
didn't even know if I was going to make it. It seems so funny
to me now. I run three or four quarters in a workout and
I'll knock them off in 50 seconds like nothing, no strain at
all.*

*Next day, starting off with the hurdles, I kept thinking
about what had happened to me at the Dickinson Relays
the week before. I thought, if that happens to me again, I'm
going to just die. But I three-stepped the first flight and the
next one and the one after that. I kept thinking, I'm doing
it, I'm doing it. And I did. I three-stepped every one and
ran a 16.2.*

His best throw in the discus was 127 feet. He vaulted 13-6,
and threw the javelin 199 feet. Those marks seem paltry
when set against his performance at Montreal, but for a
first-time try at the decathlon, his scoring was phenomenal.
His projection of 7,000 points was within reach if he could run
a respectable 1500 meters. Some college athletes struggle for
years to reach that plateau. Jenner had scored well enough to
be four points ahead of a teammate, Bob Hutchins, with the
1500 meters still to be run.

*Hutchins was a cocky guy, a pretty good athlete, and he'd
spent most of the last month telling me how hard the
decathlon was going to be and how I didn't stand a chance
of beating him. I couldn't argue with him, and I told him
so. I didn't know what it was all about. But I kept thinking,
boy, it sure would be nice to beat him. He'd been giving me
such a hard time.*

We were in different heats of the 1500. He ran before I

did, and finished in 4:51. That gave me something to shoot at. I'd never run that far in my life. I don't remember my pace, but I do know that it felt like I was running my guts out on the last lap. I ran a 4:39, set a school record of 6,991, beat Hutchins by 75 points, and finished sixth. He was seventh. And that was the best part, because the first six finishers all got nice awards. The seventh-place guy didn't win a thing.

When the meet was over, I told myself that I'd found something that I wanted to do. I decided to run cross-country and get in shape for the decathlon. It was so much fun, such a challenge, and I was encouraged, because I'd done so well in a couple of events and had come so close to scoring 7,000. But what appealed to me most was that it was all on me—not like any of the team sports, where you can play your best game and still lose because some other guy plays like he doesn't care. Whatever I did in the decathlon, good or bad, was a product of my own work and ability.

Jenner ran a second decathlon that spring, at the NAIA (small college) national meet. He scored over 6,800 points, finished third behind Bennett and Gary Hill, and won a certificate as a small-college All-American decathlete. The next winter he ran cross-country races and trained on the 220-yard oval inside the Graceland gymnasium. The first meet of the season—this was now the spring of 1971—came at the Kansas Relays. Bennett, who had won the only two decathlons that Jenner had previously entered, didn't show for this one. But Hill did.

I wanted so much to go over 7,000. Going into the 1500, I was about 50 points up on Hill and thinking about this beautiful gold watch that the winner of the decathlon was going to get. To make up 50 points in the 1500, Hill had to beat me by eight seconds. I figured he could. My best time was the 4:39 I ran my first time out. Hill's p.r. was 4:25. But we ran in the same heat and I decided I would get in behind him, just zero in on his back, and not let him get away. We went through the half mile at 2:17, which even today is a good pace for me. I was just looking at his back, holding on. On the last lap, he started to move. He was just flying down the backstretch and I could hear his coach on the sidelines yelling, "You got him, Gary, you got him." I was doing all I could to stay close, and I was running so hard that I didn't know if I could make it around the turn. He pulled maybe two or three yards ahead of me in the stretch but I caught him in the turn again. I was right behind him, just behind his right shoulder, when he turned his head to see how far behind I was. When he saw me there, right with him, he just slowed down and I ran past him. Later he told me that he'd never heard me, that he figured he had left me in the dust somewhere back there on the turn. Anyway, I ended up beating him by eight seconds, ran a 4:25, and scored 7,330.

I was encouraged. I was doing well at something I liked, which was all the reinforcement I needed to work even harder. By now I'd figured out that the harder I worked, the more points I would score. That was all I needed to know, because I wanted those points. That's what I lived for. Munich, Montreal, the world record, I wasn't thinking about that. That seemed too far away from what I was doing. I didn't know enough about the event and what other people were doing to put myself in any kind of perspective. I knew I was pretty good, and that was all I cared about. Getting to the top, being the best, never occurred to me. I took my 7,330 and was happy with it.

For every Thorpe, Johnson, and Jenner there is at least one L. D. Weldon. He coaches, counsels, sometimes bullies, sometimes babies his athletes. The hours are long, the pay generally bad. Young athletes can be headstrong, impatient, and notoriously ungrateful. But the coaches are there anyway, on playing fields and in gymnasiums, turning kids now and again into superstars. Bob Mathias had never heard of the decathlon until his coach at Tulare (California) High School, a man named Virgil Jackson, urged him to enter a meet in Los Angeles in 1948. Five months later, Mathias was the Olympic decathlon champion.

L. D. Weldon recognized talent in Jenner and turned him into a competitor. "He was the ideal athlete," Weldon says now. "Never gave me a bit of lip, never any trouble. Even when I'd make a mistake, he'd never throw it up to me the way some of them might."

Weldon knew the decathlon. Maybe he didn't talk in all the latest physio-kinetic jargon, but he knew athletic potential and he saw it in Jenner. He had coached Jack Parker, bronze medal winner behind Glenn Morris in 1936. He had turned out a series of accomplished decathletes at Sacramento City College and later at Graceland.

"There were other athletes," he says, "with more talent than Jenner. Mike Mattox, the kid who roomed with Jenner, was bigger and faster than Bruce. But he hated the weight room. Bruce, though, I told him what he needed to do and he did it. He was a coach's dream. You could stand off to one side and watch him get better, one meet after another."

I was working hard and loving it. I was curious to see what my limits were, to see just how good I could be. So few people have that chance, to find out how good they can be in any undertaking. They're more concerned with day-to-day things that obscure what they're trying to do. They don't have long-range goals or the means to measure how well they're succeeding at those goals.

A week after he beat Hill, Jenner scored over 7,400 to finish second to Rick Wanamaker in the Drake Relays. He topped 7,500 a month after that at a Kansas Invitational meet. Then he spent the winter running, lifting weights, and thinking of 7,600 points. That was the next logical plateau. It was also the minimum required for an invitation to the U.S. Olympic Trials the next summer. Surely, with all the work he had invested over the winter, that 7,600 would come in the first meet of the season. Again it was the Kansas Relays. But for the first time, the equation failed. More work didn't equal more points. He barely reached 7,300. Then he ran at Drake the next week.

I was down. I couldn't understand it. I began to think, well, this is it, this is as far as you're going to get. I'd been trying to find my limits and maybe this was it. And it got worse the first day at Drake. I ran a slow 100. I had a terrible long jump. I had three lousy throws in the shot. By this time I was ready to cry. I'd put in all this work over the winter and I was going downhill, worse than I'd done the year before. But one of the things I'd been working on was the Flop in the high jump. So I went out to high-jump and it worked: I flopped 6-4, a new p.r., and that made me feel better. Then I ran a good quarter. And I finished that first day with 3,700, not so great but still respectable. And everything worked the second day. I had a lucky javelin throw of 227 feet, which was my p.r. for four years until I just barely beat it at the Trials in 1976. I ran 4:24 in the 1500 and that put me over—7,678.

That was his ticket to the Olympic Trials in Eugene. Bennett and Jeff Bannister, the two top American decathletes that year, were virtually conceded two of the three spots on the U.S. team. The third was still in doubt, but Jenner had to be considered one of the less likely candidates among the contenders.

"Before we went to the Trials," Weldon recalls, "I told him that he had a chance, an outside chance. I said if he could stay close going into the 1500, he might be able to do it. I figured he could take nine or ten seconds off his own best time in the 1500 if he had to do it to make the team."

I estimated that I'd have to score over 7,900, and the best I'd ever done was the 7,678 at Drake that got me there in the first place. I didn't expect I'd make it, and nobody else did, either. That had to be an advantage. The only time I had ever run against most of those honchos was in the AAU (Amateur Athletic Union) Nationals the year before, and I was terrible then. I didn't make a height in the high jump or the pole vault. Everybody running at the Trials had been there at the Nationals, too. I didn't figure they'd be taking me too seriously.

I had a good meet. But I was in tough company and I was in eleventh place after the first day. By the second day I picked up one place here, another place there, and all of a sudden I'm in fifth place going into the 1500. Steve Gough was in third, Fred Samara was fourth. But when we went out to run the race, I looked at those two guys and I knew I had it won. Samara didn't look like he could run another step. And Gough was sitting on a bench with his head in his hands. I thought, I've got him. I know I can beat him. I was out there, bouncing around the track, ready to run. I had to beat Gough by eighteen seconds to make the team. At the half-mile mark, he was still with me. So I started running faster and I just flat left him behind. I beat him by 21 seconds, ran the fastest 1500 I ever had, 4:16.9. That was eight seconds faster than my old p.r. I'd never been happier.

He had been such a long shot that his parents had decided not to travel to Eugene to watch him compete. So he ran to a telephone to call them while he was still out of breath from the race.

"He was so excited," his mother says, "but he made Bill come to the extension phone so that he could tell us both.

And Bill, I thought he was going to have a heart attack, he was so excited."

It's amazing the way people's attitudes toward you change when you start reaching the upper levels of the sport. For example, the day before the competition I finally got up enough nerve to ask the man from Puma for a free pair of shoes. He gave me a pair of sprint shoes, the first pair of shoes I hadn't bought for myself. I felt pretty proud. Not fifteen minutes after I'd run the 1500 and made the team, Adidas told me to show up the next day at the hotel, that they would fix me up. That's how I spent the next day, collecting shoes. I was in heaven, two bags full of free shoes.

Banners, TV cameras, and friends from Graceland and Lamoni were waiting when Jenner arrived at the airport in Des Moines several days later. He had never seen anything like it. But a lot of things were beginning to change. Jenner remembers that the Des Moines media had neglected him in favor of Rick Wanamaker, an Iowa native who had gone to the Trials with much more impressive credentials: He had been the 1970 collegiate champion at Drake and had won the 1971 Pan-Am Games and AAU championships.

It was always Rick this, Rick that, everywhere you looked on TV and in the papers. He'd won the big meets and he was also a native, which helped. I was an import, and besides I went to this tiny school. But it still got to me.
When I got off the plane at Des Moines, one of the TV people wanted to do an interview. Just before we started filming, he told me, "Let's say something nice about Rick." He started the interview by building Rick up until he was nothing short of Thorpe. Then he finally turns to me and says, "Well, what do you think about Rick?" I was tempted, let me tell you. I wanted to say, "I'm going to Munich and

he's not." But I didn't. I just said what a shame it was that
he hadn't made the team.

A photograph taken in Munich a few days before the decathlon shows Bruce with his college girl friend, Chrystie. In six
months they would marry. They are smiling the triumphant
grins of a couple of kids who have managed to sneak into the
circus. They are dressed like American college kids, circa
1972: inexpensively, haphazardly, with hair shaggy. And the
contrast between the Jenner of Montreal and this boy in
Munich is perhaps the best testimony to the long hours he
would lavish on his body during the intervening years. For
there is nothing to suggest the athlete here except a good set
of wide shoulders. The legs are skinny and the torso is spare.
There is no hint that he is anything but one of so many
thousands of American college boys enjoying a summer ad-
venture in Europe with his blonde girl friend.

Which, in a sense, is exactly what this was—a sight-seeing
trip to the greatest athletic spectacle of all, except that he had
earned an especially advantageous seat. Neither he nor anybody else expected Jenner to win this meet, and this time he
didn't surprise anyone. He was the third man on a three-man
U.S. team. There were at least a dozen athletes better known
and better prepared. Or, more precisely, he was one of
perhaps two dozen who were virtually unknown outside a
small circle of decathlon fanatics. He was along for the ride, to
take in the sights and to run the decathlon simply for the sake
of doing it.

And it happened that he saw a lot more than anyone had
expected.

The day before the decathlon, I was in the bathroom
brushing my teeth when Steve Prefontaine, one of my
roommates, came into the room from a morning run and
told me that somebody had been killed in the village. I went
out to have breakfast and kept hearing more and more

about it. Then I saw all the soldiers and the riot squads and the tanks. It was quite bizarre. I'd never been exposed to anything like that before. It was like something out of a movie. I knew some athletes in the Puerto Rican section, which was right across the way from the Israeli compound. The Puerto Ricans had a trainer who gave great rubdowns, so I pretended to go up there for a rubdown. I went out to the balcony of the seventh floor and looked out over to the Israeli dorm, maybe a hundred yards away. We could see rifles sticking up, and every so often one of the terrorists would stick his head out and look around. At the time, I guess I didn't grasp all the implications of it. It was hard to realize that I was standing next to the biggest news story in the world, and that what was going on would affect every Olympics to come.

It was very disillusioning to me. I had an image of what the Olympics was supposed to be, the ideal of all the greatest athletes in the world getting together for the sake of competition. But in reality it was turning out so much different.

I was angry and I was bugged, too. It took me a while to admit that to anyone, but I was mad that these Arabs had come along and killed people and were cheating me out of my Olympics. The next morning, when the decathlon was supposed to have started, all the sports were suspended for a funeral for the Israelis who had died. I felt sorry for the athletes and their families. But I was also annoyed that these terrorists had come along, used the Olympics for their own political purposes, and were disrupting what I had been looking forward to for so long. I was afraid to admit that to anyone for a long time. You have to realize how much time I'd spent getting there, how much it meant to me to be a part of it.

When we finally did run the decathlon, I ended up with some good events and some bad ones. I was happy to finish tenth. I was in the stands watching when the scores came *up on the big board. There was Avilov way ahead of everybody else with his world record, 8,454, then Leonid Litvinenko and Ryszard Katus and Bennett, and finally there was Jenner in tenth place, 7,722.*

Frank Zarnowski is an economics professor at Mount St. Mary's College in Emmitsburg, Maryland. He may also be this country's reigning expert on the decathlon. He was in the stands at Munich and filmed the events with a home movie camera. After he had watched Jenner in Montreal, he replayed those films from Munich.

"I wasn't impressed by him at Munich," he says, "but when Jenner got so good in the next couple of years, I thought I must have missed something. So I took a look at the old film and found out that I was right the first time. He was a good athlete but there were a lot of others who were better. There was nothing there to suggest what he would be accomplishing in the next couple of years. He just didn't look that good. Physically, he's a different person now than he was then. In those old films, he looks skinny. He says he hasn't gained much weight in the last four years, but I can't believe it. That's just not the same body."

I thought a lot about it. I knew I could do better. I felt I had potential far better than that. How much better, I didn't know. I knew that I had an advantage, just having been here at Munich and having been exposed to it all. It's so big and imposing that it awes you the first time around. There's so much going on that it's hard to concentrate. But now that I'd seen it once and done it all, maybe I'd be able to ignore the distractions the second time.

I thought it over for a while. I wasn't ready to quit. Four years would make me 26 years old, put me right at my peak. So I decided to move to California, commit all my energy to the next four years, and do all that I could to win the gold medal.

50

It was, perhaps, a last step into adulthood. Gone was the pleasant boyhood illusion of everlasting youth. He saw limits to his time and energy. He knew that the next four years would be his body's best, and he knew that so many other men his age would be using that abundance of young men's energy to start families and advance careers. He knew all that. And still he decided to use those four years to pursue what anyone else would have considered a reckless long shot.

His life would never be the same.

A Life Apart

Esther Jenner recalls "he was a muscular little fellow when he was two-years old. He had a big chest and big, wide shoulders. We called him 'Bruiser.'"

The sweat suit that twelve-year old Jenner is wearing says U.S. Olympic Goof Off Champ.

Part of the Jenner family poses for a portrait on a visit to Ohio. Bruce (age eight); his mother, Esther; his father, Bill; and sister Pam.

Fifteen-year old Bruce competing in the Boys' Jumping Event at the Eastern Regional Championship at Reading, Pa.

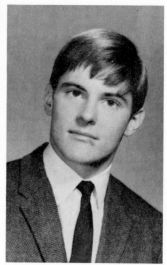

High School graduation
picture, 1968, Newtown, Conn.

A happy teenager holds his trophies won
at a water skiing event at Endicott, N.Y.

As a sixteen-year old junior at Sleepy Hollow High School in Tarrytown,
N.Y., Bruce was a better-than-average defensive football player.

Practicing for the slalom event at Canton, Conn., in 1969.

By eighteen, Bruce had accumulated a few trophies—mostly in
water-skiing, track and field, football and basketball.

Training sessions at the San José City College athletic field, Fall 1975.

Working with weights at the San José Y.M.C.A. in preparation for the Olympics. His personal best in the Clean & Jerk was 270 pounds.

Training sessions at the San José City College athletic field, Fall 1975.

One night during the spring of 1976 Jenner watched a television film documentary about the history of the decathlon in the Olympic Games. It was a thorough work that included some film footage Jenner had never before seen. He was thoughtful the next morning when he talked about it.

May 13, 1976

I got very much into the show, imagining myself being there. I really got into watching people like Thorpe and Mathias, even though their technique was so much different from the styles now. I could identify much more easily with Rafer and Toomey, because they're much closer to my era.

I felt funny watching these fellows, knowing that they once went through exactly the same thing that I'm going through, ten weeks before the Games. They were just as nervous and intense as I am.

You look at these films, people like Thorpe, Mathias, Rafer, they look like such superstars. And then I remind myself, hey, little old me sitting in front of the TV, I can do everything they ever did. Better. But I feel the same inside. These guys are my heroes. I've reached the level of my

55

*heroes yet nothing has changed inside me. I'm the same guy
I was when I was in junior high school. I haven't changed
any. I'm bigger and stronger and older, but the person
inside of me is the same as it ever was. I'm confronted by
that same thing when I'm introduced to strangers these
days. They look at me and they see a world-record holder.
They think I'm something special. But I'm the same old guy
I always was, always have been. Same old hangups and
problems.*

His image of an adolescent boy inside a mature body seems
apt. There is a lot of boy in the man who won the gold medal.
To be more precise, there is little evidence in him of the
psychological complications often associated with adulthood.
He is a remarkably honest and basic man. He takes genuine
pleasure in his home, his wife, and his dog. He is open and
affable to strangers, and, as a result, he has a great number of
social acquaintances. He also has a very few friends; to these,
I believe, he will be perpetually loyal. These qualities are
trite, and so are his faults. But Jenner offers no apologies and
neither do I. This is the man he is, and he has been this way
too long to begin assuming pretensions simply for realism's
sake.

All this is true as far as it goes. But talking about the
decathlon introduces another dimension. Jenner in pursuit of
his gold medal was capable of things that the little boy inside
could never countenance. There was a joke being told at the
Olympic Trials in June 1976 that was supposed to illustrate
the distance runners' dedication to their sport.

"Tell a distance runner that eating manure will increase his
endurance," the line went, "and the next morning you'll have
a bunch of skinny guys lined up outside the stable with plates
in their hands."

It could as easily—probably more truthfully—have been
applied to Jenner. In the cause of the gold medal, almost no
excess would have been too great. Though intelligent, he is

hardly an intellectual; but if he believed that the secret of the perfect javelin throw lay within the original *Iliad*, he would have learned to read ancient Greek and would have memorized every word. Though friendly by nature, he would have forced himself to become surly and nasty if doing that could have brought him any closer to the object of his pursuit. Probably he would have stopped at murder. Probably. Still, I would not have wanted to stand between him and the finish line of the 1500-meter race at Montreal. I would not have wanted to try to stop him from crossing that line.

I agree with most of what Finch has to say. But that's part of me. I'm agreeable. I'm easy. There's only one point where he misses the mark. He implies I might have killed somebody who tried to stop me from crossing the finish line at the end of the 1500 meters in Montreal. Wrong. I would have run around him. That's a lot more my way, to avoid conflict if at all possible.

Now, writing after his victory, after he has left athletics, I find him strangely difficult to grasp. It is as though he is waiting for another undertaking to supply him with form and definition as the decathlon did. Perhaps one day he will be the quintessential television commentator, just as he trained himself to be the quintessential decathlete. I know that to understand the decathlon was to understand Jenner. He grew in some ways and shrank in others to conform exactly to the sport. He and it were inextricably linked in my mind because he talked and thought about so little else. To have been so close to it for so long until the climax at Montreal must be as close as he ever will come to experiencing maternity and childbirth. I wonder if he feels anything like the post-partum blues.

June 10, 1976

It may take two weeks, two years, but I'll have to find something else when this is all over, something that means as much to me as the decathlon. Some people have talked to me about television or movies. Maybe that's a good idea, maybe not. I've got pride. I'm not going to do something unless I'm good at it, comfortable with it. I'm not going to stand in front of a camera and make a fool of myself. Whatever it turns out to be, I've got to have something to keep climbing for. I'm going to have a lot of problems if I come home from Montreal and sit on my hands for the rest of my life.

It will have to be a solitary undertaking. I doubt that he could be happy very long in a situation for which he did not bear total responsibility. He is accustomed to relying on himself for strength and resource. Having his own success or failure in another's hands would be impossible for him to accept. He has been conditioned by the solitary life of an athlete.

It is a life that sets a man apart from the rest of the world. It is a life bounded and defined by readings on a stopwatch, by the precise and orderly markings on a running track. As he immersed himself in the decathlon, Jenner became more and more an alien in everyday life. His needs and his wants, the strict parameters of his success, and his extraordinary dedication to his goal, all separated him from the world that most of us know and understand.

And he realized it. He knew that he was different from the rest of us. He felt it vividly the day before he was to compete at Montreal, when he and his wife drove out of the city for lunch at a lodge in the nearby mountains.

There were people all around us, having lunch. They were laughing and having a good time. They had no conception of what I was about to do or what I had been going through. For them, the next day was going to be just another day. For me, my whole life would be determined by what I did in the next 24 hours. I got a real feeling of how different my life had been, of how I'd been living in a world of my own.

I often felt that people who aren't heavily into athletics couldn't identify with what I was going through. Some of our friends didn't care about athletics at all, and we got along fine, but they never really saw me in the area where I was at my best. I was just Bruce, the guy who sat around the house a lot and came home sweaty in the evenings. Even when they saw me in my sweat clothes, I don't think they realized the work that was going on. Within that circle of people, people I knew who had never seen me perform until Montreal, the television coverage of the Games really had an impact. They were seeing me at my best for the first time. They look at me a lot differently, even now that I'm back in that original context, here in my living room where they always knew me.

The life of an athlete is so different. It can be a pain. A normal person wakes up with a crick in his back and just forgets about it. With me, that was something to worry about. You're so concerned with your body, always watching it and worrying about it and thinking about it. I worried about my diet. I worried about standing in a draft or being on my feet too long. I worried about every little twinge. It was a strange experience, the first time I played tennis after Montreal. I'd been playing for a while when I felt a little cramp in one of my leg muscles. My first instinct was to say, whoa, better sit down and rest. Then I realized: I don't have to worry about that stuff any more. I can play as long as I want. If I end up pulling a muscle, fine, then I'll walk around with a sore leg for a few days. But it's no disaster. My life isn't my legs and my body any more. All I need my legs for now is to walk around on.

But being an athlete isn't just being preoccupied with your body. It's also a matter of attitude, a very egotistical attitude that can clash with the reality of the world outside the playing field. Sometimes that was hard for me to take. Like when I was an insurance salesman, a couple of years before the Games. I was very conscious of the difference between the way people acted toward me on the field and in the office. Other athletes respected me and understood me. They knew what I had accomplished and how hard I was working. They appreciated that. But in the office, no matter how hard I worked to be recognized, there was always somebody else who needed convincing.

So you try to downplay that side of yourself. It's tough sometimes. I have an ego. I want people to respect me. I wanted them to see me at my best, doing what I'd worked so hard to be good at. There were plenty of times, walking down the street, or even working in the office, when somebody who didn't know me would treat me like dirt and I'd feel like saying, "Hey, I'm somebody. I'm good at what I do." That ego, it's always out there. You're faced with a contradictory situation because on the one hand you're trying to keep your ego down to socially acceptable levels, but on the other hand, you're trying to cultivate it to do what you have to do on the field. You have to be a conqueror out there on the field. You have to believe that you're the best. You've got to be a warrior.

That is the essence of the solitary life Jenner chose for himself. It was an ordered, precise, ascetic life. He made his own challenges, and when he had met those challenges he created some more. It was a life of discipline and deliberate action. It left no possibility for self-delusion because it was open to scrutiny and measurement; the stopwatches do not lie, the tables have no charity. Life was a series of p.r.'s, and none was ever quite good enough.

He became a man remarkably similar to the "warrior" described by the Indian sorcerer Don Juan in Carlos Castaneda's *Journey to Ixtlan*:

"The warrior . . . is a hunter. He calculates everything. That's control. But once his calculations are over, he acts. He lets go. That's abandon. A warrior is not a leaf at the mercy of the wind. No one can push him; no one can make him do things against himself and his better judgement. A warrior is tuned to survive, and he survives in the best of all possible fashions."

That is as good a description as any of Bruce Jenner's life as he prepared for Montreal. It was as tight and compact and streamlined as he could make it. He did nothing without purpose. He had determined the best way to proceed and then he gave himself up to it. It was, truly, a warrior's life. Perhaps it is a contradiction—and perhaps not—that there was a place for a wife within that existence.

It was possible because she was everything he was not. She fit. She was tough and uncompromising and realistic in situations where he was pliable and passive. There evolved a curious division of responsibility. He had undisputed control over the only matter which really concerned him, the decathlon. The rest was hers. She balanced the checkbook and ran the house and cooked the meals and brought home most of the money, though Bruce is proud of having held part-time jobs during a good part of the four years between Munich and Montreal. She also stood between him and some of the more unreasonable demands on his time. She was good at that. She was The Enforcer. More than once, she spoke up to reporters who wanted too much at the wrong time, or to organizers of benefit dinners who had found easy pickings in Bruce and had nearly talked him into commitments he really shouldn't have made. Bruce needed that kind of help.

They met for the first time when both were freshmen at Graceland, but they were only casual friends then. Chrystie became engaged to someone else that semester, left school, then broke the engagement one month before the wedding.

61

Bruce was in his junior year when she returned to Graceland. He immediately asked her out the first day of school. They went to a movie, and while they were standing in line, one of Chrystie's acquaintances spotted her and the handsome, if boyish, young man beside her.

"She came running over and gave me a hug like we were old friends," Chrystie says now. "She had a date, too, and the first thing she said was that we all should sit together. But somehow she ended up sitting next to Bruce. I kept talking to Bruce, trying to distract him, but I guess it was the wrong thing to do."

Bruce claims that his only recollection of the evening is that his date, the girl named Chrystie, seemed to have a tough time following the plot of the movie because she kept asking him questions. When he took her to her dormitory, Bruce bolted away from the door without kissing her goodnight. They did not date again. Bruce began to go out with the girl who had sat on the other side of him during the movie.

Finally, when they returned to school the next year, he and Chrystie began dating often, and seriously. Chrystie, living in an apartment with three other women, lost a roommate. Jenner knew an opening when he saw one. He was living in the basement of L. D. Weldon's home, but his clothes and books kept disappearing from there and began cluttering the closets of Chrystie's apartment. If Weldon was less than enthusiastic about the propriety of the arrangement, he could not argue with the results. Jenner made the dean's list those two semesters for the first time. Neither Bruce nor Chrystie will say how directly she helped his studying, but it is now a household joke that if they should ever divorce, there may be a nasty argument over who gets custody of Bruce's diploma.

"It was a weird time," Chrystie says. "I literally could not use the words husband, wife, children, or marriage when I was around Bruce. He didn't want to hear about it. That made talking about married couples pretty difficult. The only exception I can remember was when we talked about another decathlete who was training in Lamoni while his wife worked in another city to support him. Bruce said that he had no respect for anyone who would live under that arrangement. He said that he could never let his wife totally support him. I said I thought it was a good arrangement, except for the fact that the husband and wife in this case weren't living together. But I didn't at all mind the idea of a wife working to let the husband have the freedom to do something that was important to him."

She was persuasive, and so were the demands of the decathlon. A year later, when the newlyweds moved to San Jose, California, so that Bruce could train more seriously, it was with the understanding that she would continue as a stewardess (she had begun her training for that job three semesters short of a degree from Graceland) and that he would work only when a job did not interfere with his workouts.

But that first year was a bad one. He injured his back in competition. He despaired.

"I walked out on him twice," she says. "Without the training, he had nothing. He was as bad as the old stereotype of the lazy housewife who does nothing during the day but change the channels on the TV so that she can watch her soap operas. That was Bruce. It didn't bother me that he wasn't training or that he wasn't working, but that he was doing absolutely nothing. One day he asked me to help him find a hobby. I thought that was sad, really pathetic. It was so unlike him. We kept reading the Help Wanted section of the classified ads and finally found an opening for somebody with experience climbing trees, as he had done for his dad. That made things a lot better."

When he began training again, she learned how jealous he could be of his domain on the track.

"I knew a lot about the decathlon," she says, "but Bruce wouldn't listen when I had something to say. He would argue over some little statistic or point when I knew I had it right. It

63

took me a while to realize that this was his, that he didn't want anybody interfering. My expertise in anything else was fine. He didn't care that much about anything but the decathlon."

So Bruce took care of the dream, and she tended to the details. She saw for the first time how intense and single-minded he could be.

"At Graceland, he was serious," she says, "but he always left it on the field. It didn't dominate his life. When we were together, we talked about other things. Once we got to San Jose, he became so obsessed with the decathlon that it was hard to communicate with him on any other level. Usually, his eyes would glaze over and he wouldn't answer me, and I knew he was thinking about the decathlon."

Success introduced a new set of problems. Because the decathlon was so exclusively his responsibility, the victory was his own, too. In 1975 Chrystie began treatment under a psychiatrist and joined a women's therapy group.

"I kept going back and forth between two extremes. Part of the time I was trying to get my own vicarious satisfaction out of Bruce's accomplishments, living my life through him, which was wrong. Then I would overreact and tell myself that I ought to totally ignore everything that Bruce was doing and to concentrate on finding satisfaction inside myself, which would have been just as wrong. Finally I learned that maybe it wasn't such a bad idea to put my own needs second to Bruce's for a while as long as I wasn't being pushed into it, as long as I was doing it of my own accord, of my own will, and I knew it was temporary.

"Bruce was good about it. He understood, and he made a conscious effort to include me in all of his successes."

I was aware of what Chrystie was going through. Sometimes I think the problem wasn't as much with me as with other people. In a new social situation people would be climbing all over me and ignoring her. It made her feel bad, and when we were alone I would tell her that if anybody is that shallow, it's their problem, not hers. In competition, I wanted to include her. After I broke the world record the first time in Eugene, I ran over to her and kissed her and told her, "We did it. We!" I really felt that way.

Other women put her in an awkward position sometimes, coming on to me. I don't have a lot of experience with women. Until I met Chrystie, I dated no more than four or five girls for any length of time. I was pretty shy. If a woman gives me a come-on, it has to be awfully overt or I won't even know it. A raised eyebrow or some other subtlety is generally lost on me. But Chrystie knows. When I find out about it, I try to tell her how much she has going for her and that she has no competition at all, which is true.

"What hurts me," she says, "are the women who come up to Bruce to hug him or kiss him as though I weren't there. I think it's degrading to me. It's disrespectful. If a woman comes to me first and says, 'Do you mind if I kiss your husband?' I don't mind nearly as much. That's a lot different. As far as women making a really serious play for Bruce, I think there's surprisingly little of that going on. And I think I'd know it if I saw it. I guess Bruce doesn't have that kind of appeal. He's more the Huck Finn type. Women want to mother Huck Finn, not romance him."

I don't know if I could have done it, winning the gold medal, without Chrystie. It's hard to speculate. People change so much in marriage and I can't say what kind of person I would be now if I had stayed single. My life would have been a lot different. I'd have lived with a bunch of guys, probably would have spent too much time running around instead of staying at home, and sure would have had a tougher time financially. Chrystie definitely made things easier.

I know I'm independent, a survivor. It helped us both

that she was able to travel to all the meets with her airline privileges. A lot of athletes have trouble in their marriages because they're always running off to meets around the world while the wife stays at home. They come back home a week later, tell the wife, "Boy, what a great meet I had, what a lot of fun," and they throw a few clippings and some picture postcards down on the table. That's tough.

"I've wondered about it," she says. "I've wondered how it would have been without me. Bruce tells me that he couldn't have done it without me, but I think he's trying to make me feel good. He's such a self-sufficient person, I can't see him relying on anybody for crucial help, not even his wife. That's not his way. I think he would have found a way somehow, I really do. He's that kind of person."

**The Way in
San Jose**

Bruce Jenner and Chrystie Crownover were married December 16, 1972. They had no furniture and no home. She had left school by this time to train as a stewardess for United Airlines, when she sensed that her husband-to-be would not be donning a three-piece worsted and trotting off to an office the day after his graduation. She arranged for assignment to New York City, the plan being that Bruce would find a home somewhere in Connecticut. But he was bound to a term of teaching in a Lamoni high school before Graceland would send him on his way with a diploma in physical education. So they lived in Lamoni. Rather, Bruce lived in Lamoni and Chrystie spent most of her time commuting between New York and Iowa.

The new life was off to a fitful start. He wanted to be in California with his wife, training for the decathlon. But Jenner tells a story which may show that his mind—if not his body—was in the right place.

It was during a Christmas break. I'd gone back home and I was working for my dad to make some extra money. I'd done this all my life, at least part-time. I used to climb trees, cut branches, never thought anything about it. But

69

this day my dad took me out to an emergency call. The top of a tree had broken off and had fallen on the branches. Right below the limb that it was laying on were high-tension wires, real big ones. Touch one and you fry. And below those wires was a big rock wall. My job was to climb the tree, go way out on the limb, cut up the piece that was laying on the branches, and then throw it down. It was cold, the middle of winter, and we were right on the side of a frozen lake, with the wind blowing off the ice. I don't remember what kind of tree it was, but I do know that it was a brittle one. The worst part was that since the whole top of the tree had broken off, there was nothing up above me to secure a rope to so that I'd have something to catch me if I fell. I climbed up to the top, up to that branch, and there was nothing up above me but the big grey sky.

I started edging out on the limb. It started creaking, making all kinds of noises. I thought it was ready to go. So I edged my way back to the trunk and looked at it for a couple of minutes, and after due consideration, I decided I wasn't doing it.

My dad had gone to another job. He'd left me with another guy, a buddy of mine. I told my buddy that I wasn't going out there, and that he ought to be the one to do it. No way, he said, he wouldn't go out there either. So we sat in the truck to warm up and we started to think up excuses to tell my dad when he got back.

Which he did, before too long. He stopped his car and looked at me with this what-are-you-doing-in-the-truck kind of look. I got out and I told him he could say what he wanted but I wasn't going out on that limb. He started to laugh. He said, "Bruce, don't do this to yourself. You'll never live it down. As long as you live, you'll never live this down."

I told him I didn't care, that I had too much at stake and that I'd never be able to train if I fell out of that tree and broke my back.

That really gave him a laugh. "My whole business is at stake," he said, "and you're just worried about whether you're going to be able to run." He climbed the tree, still in his shirt and tie, went out to the end of the limb, and cut it all down, a beautiful job. And still wearing a shirt and a tie, too, just to rub it in. He still gives me a hard time about that, but I don't care. I'm still not sorry I didn't go out on that limb.

By the spring of 1973 San Jose was beginning to earn a reputation as a track town. Sprint champions John Carlos, Lee Evans, and Tommy Smith had attended San Jose State College. Al Feuerbach, one of the top shot-putters in the world, had become the first of what would become a parade of world-class weight specialists to make their home there in the Santa Clara Valley. Until that time, Los Angeles had been the undisputed track center of the state. But San Jose, in the middle of the Santa Clara Valley, 60 miles south of San Francisco, was cleaner and less frantic than Los Angeles. The training facilities at San Jose City College and at San Jose State College were at least adequate. And though winters could be wet, they weren't frigid. Word got around: San Jose was a good place to train and live if you happened to be an aspiring or accomplished track and field athlete. They came in such quantity and quality that by 1976 John Powell and Mac Wilkins were trading the world discus record from one side of town to the other, two of the top three decathletes in the nation (Samara and Jenner) were sharing the weight room at the YMCA, and a local sports columnist had calculated that the Santa Clara Valley, as a separate nation, would have finished fifth in the final medal standings at Montreal, behind only the USSR, East Germany, the United States, and West Germany.

"He had gone about as far as he was going out here," Weldon said recently in Iowa. "He needed San Jose. He needed serious training all year round and he needed exposure to the really good athletes. He was ripe, just ready to explode. He was a great athlete just waiting to happen."

So, after Jenner received his diploma from Graceland in the spring of 1973, he and Chrystie came to San Jose looking for a place to live.

We spent a couple of weeks out here looking for a decent apartment that we could afford. We kind of stumbled into what we finally settled on. It was perfect, at least for my purposes. Right next to the track at City College. I couldn't get away from my training if I wanted to. If I had trouble getting started in the morning, I just looked out of my bedroom window at the running track. There it was out there—my destiny. I really felt that way.

It was exactly the sort of apartment that any newly married couple on a strict budget would have chosen. It was on the top floor of a cluster of three-story buildings, plain but at least clean. The furnishings, though, were unique: 16-pound iron shot used for a doorstop; vaulting poles lying behind the couch, against the only wall long enough to accommodate them; closets full of nylon sweatsuits and running shoes; a small barbell sitting on the terrace where most young Californians keep their hibachi charcoal brazier.

I got an education really quick. I'd always thought that I was strong, but very soon I found out different. The first time I went to the weight room at the YMCA, I started doing squats. That's an exercise where you squat down, take the bar on your shoulders, behind your head, hold it there, and then try to stand up from that position. I did a few and thought I was real hot stuff. Then along comes Maren Seidler, a woman shot-putter, and she out-squats me like it was nothing at all. A girl!

That kind of thing happened a lot at first. It opened my eyes. I was being exposed to a lot of stuff for the first time.

72

It's not just a matter of training harder and more often out
here in San Jose; it's a frame of mind. There are a bunch of
people out here who have made track and field their prim-
ary job. They're serious athletes.

At Graceland, I was a big athlete. Out here, I was
nobody. It seemed as if everybody out here was bigger and
faster and stronger than I was. I had to work to stay
respectable. I mean, if you have any pride at all . . . I
would bust my gut to throw 40 feet in the shot and then Al
Feuerbach would come along and put it about 60 without
even a warm-up. You see that, and you tell yourself, hey,
this is ridiculous. It made me realize how underdeveloped I
was, how much further I had to go, seeing all these guys so
much better than I was.

With that atmosphere, training all the time, with all
those specialists there to help me, I figured I had to get
better.

He had expected instant results. He was disappointed. The
athletic time bomb that Weldon had seen never came close to
exploding. He broke a foot during an indoor meet and missed
two months of training. During his first meet after he returned to action, he injured his back throwing the javelin. He
was invited to the trials for the World University Games at
Penn State University, but he walked off the track and withdrew on the morning of the first day after running 11.4 in the
100 meters and long-jumping just 20 feet, 2¼ inches.
Montreal was exactly three years and one week away.

"When he walked off the track at Penn State," Zarnowski
says, "I thought he was finished. He looked too discouraged
and he had too much against him."

I can see why Zarnowski would get that impression. Out-
wardly, I was down. But when I showed up for that meet, I
didn't expect to finish. My back was feeling terrible, and
after those two bad performances in the 100 and the long

jump I knew there was no point in going on in that particular decathlon. But I was just in the middle of moving to California about that time and I wouldn't have done that if I were giving up training. That was the whole point behind the move.

But it was a terrible year. I finished with 7,777 points for my best score of the season, and that was totally a product of all the work I'd done the year before. I wasn't making any progress. If anything, I was losing ground. I tried to think about Montreal, but that seemed so far away. At the rate I was going, I didn't even know if I'd get there at all.

Things were tight financially, too, but that would have been a lot easier to take if the training had been going well. We had very little furniture, Chrystie's salary was just barely enough, and the apartment seemed to get smaller and smaller as things got worse. I wanted to get some money coming in, so I took a job with a tree surgeon, trimming trees on the sides of the roads. I got pretty discouraged about that time. I thought, all this work, what has it got me? I'm not scoring any better, I'm not making any money, I'm 23 years old and I'm doing the same job I did when I was a teenager. What's the point?

But a series of cortisone shots relieved the pain in his back. He began selling life insurance and real estate with an acquaintance named Ron Mickle. Today, Jenner talks as though Ron Mickle owns a part of the gold medal.

I started splitting commissions with Ron. The truth is, Ron made most of the sales and let me take part of the commissions. I didn't know much about the business, but he helped me. He was interested in me and helped me along. It was a lot better than climbing trees. I didn't feel much like running at night after I'd spent all day wrestling with logs. Things started looking up. I wasn't making a ton of money but I had plenty of time to train and the training started to get better.

So did the scores. With the pain gone from his back, he had worked hard again over the winter, and once again effort began paying points. In his first meet of the season, again the Kansas Relays, he scored 8,240 points. It was the highest score in the world since Avilov's world record nearly two years earlier, and it was Jenner's first time over 8,000 points.

His next meet was the AAU National Championships. Now Jenner was aiming at Bill Toomey's meet record of 8,232 points. He stayed on pace, needed 4:15 in the 1500 meters to break the record, and pushed himself to a p.r. of 4:13, which stood until the last race of his career in Montreal. The top finishers in the AAU meet also qualified to compete for the U.S. team in a decathlon meet against the teams from West Germany and the USSR in Tallinn, Estonia.

His first-day score there, 4,146 points, put him in position to beat Avilov's world record if he could run close to his p.r.'s the second day.

I'll never forget it. Just as I was getting ready to run the hurdles the morning of the second day, a little old guy ran out of the stands, jumped out on the track, handed me a piece of paper, and went running back into the stands. I opened up the paper and looked at it. The guy had written down all the marks I'd have to make to break the world's record. He knew me pretty well, all my p.r.'s and what was realistic for me. I stuck the piece of paper in my pants without looking at it too much. I did a 14.7 in the hurdles, and he had me down for a 14.5. But I had to throw 48 meters in the discus to stay on pace and I threw 49.1 (161 feet). I thought, hmm, I'm still pretty close, so while I was waiting to pole-vault, I dug the paper out of my pocket again and took a look at it. I had to do 4.80 meters in the

*vault. That's 15-9, but the best I could do was 15-5. I
missed all three tries at 15-9 and that put me behind pace.
Then the paper had me down to do 220 in the javelin, and I
threw only 208, so I fell further behind pace. Sam Adams,
who was coaching the U.S. team, came out before the 1500
and told me that if I could run 4:03, I'd break the world's
record. He asked me if I could do it. I told him the truth: I
didn't know and I was scared to think of it.*

*The fact was, things had happened too fast for me. Just a
year before, I had been so discouraged that I was ready to
quit. It was just in the last few months that I had started to
see myself as someone who could really win the gold medal,
break the record, be the top decathlete in the world. And
that very moment, when Sam Adams came out and told me
I needed a 4:03, was the first time I had ever been able to
put it in such simple terms. In other words, I could say to
myself, this is it, all you have to do is run so-and-so and
you'll have the world's record.*

*And it scared me. You've got to be ready to be great. I
know that may sound silly, but it's true. Being on the
threshold of doing something that you've always dreamed
of doing is a very scary experience. Now that I was close
enough to get a good look at the record, it frightened me.
When you get that close, you look down inside yourself and
find out what you really want and how much you want it.
You ask yourself: Am I ready to take this one last step to be
great? Some people aren't. Since that experience, I've
talked to a lot of other athletes who have been in the same
situation, and they tell me they've had the same feeling. I
guess there's something in us that makes us afraid of
achieving our goals. Sometimes it's a lot more fun to go on
chasing.*

*Anyway, I didn't have a chance. I ran hard, but the
track was really poor. I ran a 4:22 and was happy with
that. I knew I'd be close to the record again. And I had an*

idea that the next time it happened, I would be a lot more ready to do something about it.

His winning score of 8,308 in that international meet was the highest in the world that year. Avilov had not competed because of injuries, but Jenner did beat the silver medalist at Munich, Leonid Litvinenko, by more than 450 points.

The following winter, a U.S. publication, *Track and Field News*, released its world rankings for the past season. Jenner's name led all the other decathletes. In a single season, he had improved his p.r. score by 500 points—nearly 20 percent. Such improvement is rare even among novice decathletes. At the world-class level, it would have been thought nearly impossible. Yet Jenner had done it.

What helped most was being able to train whenever I wanted while I was still working. That summer, Ron Mickle had talked to me about selling life insurance. I laughed about it at first. I didn't believe in it. I'd never bought any for myself, for sure. Ron took me in to visit a fellow from New England Life, but I didn't do anything about it for a couple of months. Then Ron quit selling real estate to sell nothing but life insurance and I figured, well, if I could work with him, maybe that wouldn't be so bad. So I started with New England Life.

It turned out to be a terrific deal. I got a salary of $700 a month to start. I didn't have to keep regular hours, just meet a regular quota every three months to keep getting the salary. The quota got bigger after a while, but it was ridiculously easy the first few months, the sort of thing you could make just by selling to family and friends. So I made my first quota in a week and I spent the next eleven weeks working out. I'd show up in the office every few days just to check out my mail and make sure I didn't have any messages. When the next quota came along, I'd work like a dog

77

*selling insurance for a week or so and then I'd be back
training again. They were good to me. I got a leave to train
for an international meet at Eugene in 1975, and I got a
six-month leave to get ready for the Games. They never
complained. The funny part is that I really got to believe in
the product. I feel as though I did people a service, selling
them life insurance. I was pretty good at it, and I could
have been a lot better.*

*We certainly needed the money. We bought furniture
for the first time and we started to live a little better. It was
still a week-to-week proposition, spending the money before it got into the bank, but at least we weren't scrimping
constantly and worrying about whether we'd run out of
money before the next paycheck.*

They even accumulated enough money for the down pay-
ment on a used Porsche 914 sports car, the least expensive
model in the line.

After four consecutive victories in 1974, he began in 1975
to string together an almost unprecedented list of successes.
On January 25, 1975, in the middle of his training season, he
won the New Zealand Games with a relatively poor score of
7,665. Four months later he won the Drake Relays again,
scoring 8,138. In June he accepted an invitation to compete
in the French Championships, mostly so that he might have a
chance to compete against Yves Leroy, who had scored over
8,000 consistently in the previous two years and who was
considered a strong contender for the gold in Montreal.
Again Jenner won, scoring 8,058 and beating Leroy by 125
points for his seventh consecutive victory.

*It wasn't a good meet. It rained all day the second day and
we vaulted into the wind with the rain blowing so hard I
couldn't keep my eyes open. But I killed Leroy in the discus
and the 1500.*

After what I'd done in 1974, I had figured I ought to get

8,500 the next year with no problem, but it wasn't happening. Then my attitude started to change. I was putting in time and effort, but I wasn't getting the results. I started telling myself, well, maybe you shouldn't put everything into this gold medal. Be a little more conservative, work a little harder on the insurance, because you may not be able to pull this thing off. I was trying to save myself from hurt when I lost. Really, I was preparing myself to lose. And only one thing can happen when you go that route. Even so, I kept on winning. One thing or another would happen and my crummy score would be good enough to win. But that couldn't go on. It had to come to an end sometime soon.

The end came in the pole-vault pit at the AAU Nationals in Santa Barbara. Just as a year earlier, the AAU championship meet also would qualify the top six finishers for the international meet against a Russian team later in the summer. Jenner scored 4,069 the first day without a single outstanding mark. He began the second day in fourth place, 213 behind the leader, Fred Dixon. Then Jenner dropped another 44 points in the hurdles, and seemed to be falling so far behind that even his advantage in the last four events might not be enough. But Dixon fouled on all three throws in the discus to drop out of contention. Jenner closed to within 100 points of the new leader, Steve Gough, and would surely take over soon—maybe even in the pole vault, where he was much stronger than Gough.

Jenner, as he usually did, relaxed on the sidelines while the weaker vaulters jumped at the lower heights. Gough equalled a p.r. by vaulting 13-9. Still Jenner passed. Then the bar moved to 14-1¼. Jenner decided that he would make his opening jumps at that height.

He had seemed strong and confident as he took has warmup jumps half an hour earlier. Of course, he always looked strong and confident; he had been vaulting since the seventh grade. Then, suddenly and without explanation, he was help-less. It was as though a stranger had been picked at random from the stands and told to pole-vault. He missed all three vaults badly. On his third attempt, he vaulted so low that he missed the bar completely, sailed beneath it and landed in the pit still holding his pole.

It was my steps. When you start vaulting, you learn a pattern of steps on your approach and you never change. That's the first thing you learn. I'd had the same steps six, eight years, and all of a sudden I lost them. I just didn't have them when I needed them. I can't explain how it happened, except that I wasn't mentally ready to run that meet. When I came down the third time without even hitting the bar, I cursed, as loud as I could, and then I threw my pole like a javelin, just missed a photographer and a TV camera—this was all on national TV. I ran off the track, ran out of the stadium, found a grove of trees and sat down in the shade. Then I started to cry. It hit me pretty hard. It had all been piling up, the pressure of the winning streak and my frustration at not being able to break the record. It all started coming out of me there. I was alone for a while, and I was glad about that. After a time, I started getting mad at myself. Then Sam Adams came over, told me not to worry, that they'd find some way of getting me on the team for the Russian meet. Chrystie came over a few minutes later. She didn't know how to react. It had been so long since I lost. She'd never seen me take it this way. I walked over to her and we started talking, the two of us alone. After a while, I felt good enough to go back into the stadium.

I was glad, in a sense, that it was all over, all the worrying and pressure of the winning streak. I'd gotten all the frustrations out of my system there under those trees. If I'd laid in the pit after I missed the jumps and kept it inside of me, it might have bugged me for years.

Chrystie and I stayed over in Santa Barbara and we talked about it. I told her about the way my attitude had been changing, that I was getting more conservative. It was strange, the way she reacted. She'd always been the one to tell me that maybe I shouldn't make it so important, that I was going to be hurt one of these days if I did. I'd always been able to convince her that this was the way I had to do it, that if I got hurt, I'd deal with it somehow.

But now that I'd gone over to her way of thinking, she turned around 180 degrees. She got mad and really gave it to me for holding anything back. She told me if I was going to do it, I'd better do it with all I had in me. We stayed up until three o'clock in the morning two nights in a row, working it out. We talked about it, how we both felt. She told me to concentrate on my running, not to worry about finances, that she would take care of that end. She was the one who convinced me not to be afraid of putting everything into winning the gold medal.

That was what I needed. I made some drastic changes. For the next month, right up to the international meet at Eugene, I cut down on my training drastically. I started training more easily, because I'd been tired in every meet, no spring in my legs at all. Instead of doing twenty crummy discus throws in an afternoon, I did three or four really good ones. I made a lot of changes in my head, too. I didn't make room for anything but winning. I wanted to score a lot of points and I wasn't afraid to admit it. I wasn't going to hold myself back. I was going to sacrifice myself to the goal, put it all on the line. This all sounds like pretty heavy inspirational stuff, but it's as close as I can come to putting into words what I felt. You really have to think in these terms if you expect to break a world record.

Jenner had one month to train for the international meet. This reduced regimen was something new. Two days out of three he sat at home or drove into the insurance company's office. Until now, he had run compulsively, believing that hard work would inevitably bring high scores. And it did, up to a point, but the returns had diminished. Now he had to convince himself that less work and more rest was the way up to that one last plateau. Now he had so much energy that he sometimes could not contain himself. Chrystie tells stories of his running hurdles while asleep, thrashing in the sheets (but three-stepping each hurdle, of course) or winding up for the discus throw while waiting in a supermarket checkout line. But when he ran—a quarter-mile every third day—he was fast. Faster than he had ever been.

The meet at Eugene was held at the same University of Oregon stadium where Jenner had qualified for the Olympic team in 1972. This meet brought together the best decathletes from the United States, Russia, and Poland. From the group of 24 competitors would almost certainly come the gold medal winner at Montreal. Avilov, who had been injured for the previous two years and had missed the meet at Tallinn, was healthy and would run. So would Litvinenko, and so would a group of talented Poles including Munich bronze medalist Ryszard Katus and Ryszard Skowronek, the 1974 European champion who had scored over 8,100 points at least once in each of the last three years. Jenner wanted badly to beat them ("as much for their benefit as for mine," he said), for Montreal now was just a year away. If he was to make himself the favorite at Montreal, in his own mind and everyone else's, this would be his chance.

He felt, he said later, "a hundred times more ready to run than I ever felt before." His remarkable sense for his body's needs and conditions was right again. He began by running the 100 meters in 10.7, a new p.r. by two-tenths of a second, scoring 50 points more than he ever had in that event. Then he met a personal goal by long-jumping 23-6¼. He was in ninth place with 1,734, but he had never scored so many points in the first two events. He moved to fourth place with a shot put of 50½ feet, and moved past Avilov into third place with a high jump of 6-7¼, his third p.r. in four events. Then he ran away from everybody in his heat of the 400 meters. That included Skowronek, who had been world-ranked second to Jenner in 1974. Jenner remembers the decathlon announcer, Frank Zarnowski, yelling over the p.a. system: "Here come Jenner and Skowronek, 1–2 in the world last year." Then, Jenner says, "I decided he would stay second." That kind of talk is typical of Jenner. If it is egotism, it is at least egotism with a basis. Because Jenner did, indeed, run away from Skowronek and from everybody else. Jenner's 48.7 moved him into second place. Only Dixon, with a 48.0 in another heat, ran the distance faster. Dixon led after the first day with 4,330. Jenner had 4,268, and a Russian named Rudolf Zigert was third with 4,245. Avilov had been strangely languid throughout, standing fifth after the first day with 4,182. He was, perhaps, something less than enthusiastic about watching a young American run at a pace that would almost certainly break his three-year-old world record. When the two men had competed once before, at Munich, Avilov put together just the same spectacular series of marks that Jenner was recording now. Jenner then was only a fresh-faced American kid with the cheek to approach Avilov after the medal ceremony, shake his hand, and tell him, "See you in Montreal, Nikolay." Now Avilov's record, which had seemed so unapproachable that afternoon in Munich, was ready to topple. And Jenner was not at all reticent about saying so.

"I don't plan to come this close to the record and then miss it," he told a gathering of reporters in an interview that evening.

The second day, he was one-tenth of a second off his p.r. in the 110-meter hurdles, at 14.6. He threw 164 feet in the discus to gain 105 points on Avilov and close to within 55 points of Dixon and the lead.

And then it was time to vault. Dixon cleared 13-9½. Jenner still had not jumped, but he grabbed a pole, walked over to a meet official, and asked to be put into the jumping rotation at 14-1¼. Dixon missed his first try at that height. So did Jenner.

I thought about what had happened at the AAU, but not too long. If I'd been that worried about making a height, I'd have started jumping when the bar was lower. But that didn't concern me. I was going for the record, and I knew I wouldn't get it if I didn't find a stiffer pole. The one I was using was the stiffest I'd brought with me, but it was still mushing out on me. I asked around, but nobody had what I needed. I made the second jump at 14-1 ¼. But I needed at least 15-5 and I wasn't going to get it with that pole.

The fiberglass poles which the vaulters use are manufactured in varying degrees of stiffness and resiliency. Their advantage over the old bamboo poles is in being able to bend in a spectacular bow and then spring back to their original shape. That spring is what allows the very best vaulting specialists to clear 18 feet and more. They literally go along for the ride when the pole snaps straight. Stiffer poles snap back harder and faster, but they also require more strength and speed to bend when the vaulter has planted the pole in the vaulting box and begun his ascent. Jenner, rested and full of energy, was overpowering his poles. The poles are graded by numbers stamped into the grip—the lower the number, the stiffer the pole. Jenner had brought his lowest-numbered pole, a 6.7 flex number, but it wasn't enough. He asked Craig Brigham, a young decathlete from the University of Oregon who was competing on his home track. Brigham couldn't help, but he remembered a pole in a metal utility shed not far away.

We started rummaging around in there. There was all kinds of junk. And one pole, lying off to a side. It was old and dusty; it looked like somebody had left it there a long time ago and forgotten it. I sort of held my breath when I turned it over. It was a 6.6, exactly what I was looking for. I grabbed it and ran back. I was thinking that if I was this lucky, there was no way I could blow the record now.

He cleared 15-1 and moved ahead of Dixon, who had missed all three attempts at 14-1¼. Jenner then flew over 15-5 on his first try before hitting the bar three times at the next height, 15-9.

After six years in the sport, Jenner knew the tables well enough. He knew that he would have to fail badly in the last two events to fall short of Avilov's record. Now he was more concerned with being the first decathlete ever to score more than 8,500 points. He calculated that he would need a throw of 215 feet in the javelin and a time of 4:15 in the 1500 meters to reach 8,500. His first try in the javelin stuck into the turf 214 feet, 11 inches from the foul line.

In the 1500, he ran away from the field. Even Litvinenko, a punishing distance runner who runs that race as well as any decathlete ever has, finished four seconds behind Jenner's 4:16.

I knew I needed a 4:26 to break the record. I took off at a good pace and started to kick in the last 440. I was running to pile up the points, put it as far out of reach as I could. I didn't know when I'd ever have that chance again.

His score: 8,524. Ironically, he had for one of the few times in his career scored fewer points the second day than the first. But his second-day total of 4,256 was still a p.r. and a world record for any decathlete on the second day of competition.

Boy, I was high. I went out running that night, just jogging, because I had so much energy. I still couldn't sleep. I was so worked up that I didn't sleep for two nights. I kept waking Chrystie up, telling her, "How about a kiss for the new world-record holder?" She got rather teed off after a while. And then I had a letdown, a natural reaction, I guess, when you've been so high. I didn't want to think about the decathlon. I didn't want to see a running track. I even wanted to take off for a while, get away, because of all the strangers who were suddenly calling the house. That lasted about two days. I woke up the morning of the third day and I couldn't wait to get out and start running again.

The mark was submitted to the International Amateur Athletic Foundation for world-record consideration and was ratified the next winter, but not without argument. Avilov's 8,454 had been compiled with automatic electronic timing in the running events. The electronic timing device in Eugene had broken down during Jenner's heat of the 100 meters and was not used again. Hand-timing can favor a score by as many as 70 to 90 points. Even after Jenner's record had been certified, there was talk that Avilov's Olympic score was a more worthy world record than the new one. Jenner usually smiled when the subject was raised. Then he would ask who had scored more points. When he signed autographs, he laboriously added the phrase, "World Record, 8,524" beneath his signature. And that was happening more often. He had become a minor celebrity in San Jose, a city that retains enough small-town naïveté to go unabashedly berserk over its local heroes.

But that enthusiasm apparently didn't extend beyond the county line. When Chrystie telephoned a San Francisco TV sportscaster to offer an exclusive interview with the new world-record holder, she was told: "We're not interested in people who go begging for publicity."

Emotionally and physically, Jenner was finished for the season. But the season was not so cooperative. He had one more meet to run, the Pan-Am Games at Mexico City, a discordant coda to a tumultuous year. Jenner was off his form, seemed bothered by the 7,000-foot altitude and by the rancor which the Latin American spectators heaped on the U.S. athletes. He narrowly beat Dixon, scoring just 8,045 to beat him by 26 points. He did come home with a gold medal, which he hung from a nail that he tacked next to the kitchen door.

Again, he was named the top decathlete of the year. But that meant little. He had more immediate concerns.

There was a sore Achilles tendon in his right leg which could cost him weeks of training time if it became aggravated. He had finally beaten Avilov but now Dixon was discovering his immense talents and scoring consistently over 8,000. Jenner had always considered Dixon a far superior athlete —superior, in fact, to almost anyone Jenner had ever seen run the decathlon. Dixon already was tough. If he learned to pole-vault and run the 1500, Jenner knew, he might be unbeatable. Jenner's world record at Eugene had not only obscured Dixon's p.r. score of 8,277, but also seven other scores over 8,000 points in that same, spectacularly productive meet.

Jenner thought about that a lot during that winter. Nine men over 8,000 points, and this from among only three nations. He thought about Dixon's fluid speed in the 400 meters and about Avilov's grace in clearing 6-10 in the high jump, even on a bad day at Eugene. He thought about his own faulty technique in the hurdles.

And those thoughts were enough to send him hurrying down the stairs and out to the track for a brisk few miles of running. There was so much work to be done. With his first meet now months away, he had no excuse for resting. Now was the time to put in the hours that would bring the points next year. Avilov would be working now. Dixon would be working now. And Jenner went to work, too.

**Six Months to
Montreal**

The winter of 1975-1976 was the driest on record in Northern California. The three-day rainstorms which usually begin arriving around Thanksgiving moved in this year after New Year's Day, and they were more like half-hour showers. That was bad for the reservoirs and for the farmers, but it was good for Bruce Jenner. That meant he stayed dry while he trudged through the daily workouts around which his life revolved. He ran 10 miles a day beginning in October. He would have run those miles in a rainstorm, but the curiously clement weather made the footing easier when he stepped off the laps at the San Jose City College track and on the Stanford University golf course.

On a routine day like today, the running begins in the morning, before breakfast. He pulls on a sweatsuit, steps down the concrete staircase of his apartment building, crosses a small asphalt parking lot, and shinnies over the high chain link fence around the City College athletic fields. The track is a bad javelin throw's distance from his apartment balcony. First his stretching exercises, loosening calves and thighs sore from yesterday's tough workout. A slow jog next, from one corner of the field to another, across a basketball court and around a softball field. The grass swishes against the soles of his running shoes. That is the only sound he hears. He is unaware of the breath that hisses through his teeth as he steps up the pace. Perspiration appears around his head, moistens his brows, slides down his nose. He stops long enough to peel his sweatsuit down to a pair of gym shorts and a T-shirt. Then out onto the track, the legs striding out, the feet skimming over the clay surface. Oh, it's a good, good feeling. Tonight he will be tired and the running will be a chore, but this morning it is a joy. His legs are strong. They carry him slap, slap, slap, down the track, devouring the ground. The kinks are gone now. The legs seem to operate independently of the rest of his body as they kick down the track. And they are so strong that the body is hardly a burden. On good mornings like this one, he almost believes that he can run this way forever. Young, strong strides . . . he feels so great . . . and the laps go ticking by. Four laps to a mile, and he can knock off ten laps this way before the pain seeps in.

There is a lot of talk about pain in distance running but it is the sort of thing that must be felt to be understood. It may appear first as a pressure in the chest, or maybe as a twinge in the back of the neck. The larynx may feel raw from the air that has been swallowed on a chilly morning. Or it may be none of these things, nothing beyond a discomfort that can only be delayed for so long, the mental strain and the physical weariness that must arrive very soon after the body has been pushed beyond its comfortable limits. If he goes on long enough, then there will be clutching-at-the-side, knife-in-the-chest, cramps-in-the-thighs pain, the kind of pain that can literally bring a strong man to his knees. But not today. Nor is it fun now, with five laps to go. Now the strides are shorter and more deliberate. Now he seems rooted to the ground, struggling to get one foot past another. The fluid motion is gone. He jerks his arms up and down, one rising as the other falls. This makes the legs move a little faster, a little more easily. He does not know why this should be true, but it is true nonetheless. So he consciously pumps his arms—the hands clenched in tight fists—to pull himself somehow around the track for one more lap, then another. He will not stop until he has run the appointed distance. To stop would be giving in to pain and to the frailty of his body. That would be setting a dangerous precedent. He is so accustomed to the pain that the urge to stop is nothing more than a tiny voice that he easily ignores.

One more lap to go and he forces himself to pump the arms faster. The legs struggle to keep pace. Push, he tells one leg. Push, to another. He forces the full length out of each stride. He is not exactly sprinting, but he is picking up the pace just the same. He is pushing the last reserve of breath out of his lungs now.

It hurts, his lungs shout.

You bet it hurts, his mind answers. It'll hurt in Montreal, too.

Now the lungs are clutching for gallons of oxygen, and getting pints. His knees no longer drive in even, precise strokes. His right shoe ticks the inside of his left calf hard enough to knock him off stride. A moment of panic: still 200 yards to go—and he has nothing left. And that turn is so wide.

Push, you SOB. Push. Off the turn. Down the straight. And drive, drive right across the line. He runs hard until he is across the line. Sometimes at this moment he imagines himself on the track in the Olympic Stadium, breasting the tape in the 1500 meters, with Avilov and Dixon far behind him. Today the desperate heaving of his lungs pushes all that aside. There is no room for fantasy.

He is quick to reach for his sweatsuit, pull on the trousers and the jacket. And while he is still panting, he trots again on the grass in a mechanical motion to keep the muscles supple.

Twice a week, in the afternoon, he goes to the eleventh green at the Stanford University golf course. That long fairway is 300 yards long, and steep. Twenty times he sprints up the hill, jogging down to the bottom each time.

But he did that yesterday, so today he has a few hours for

rest before the afternoon training. There is breakfast, a homemade granola that Chrystie periodically concocts in big batches. Then a handful of vitamin and nutrient pills: vitamin C, lecithin, B-complex, bone meal, magnesium, potassium, and kelp. In the afternoon there will be more C, some A and E, more of the minerals, the kelp, and the bone meal. At night, he repeats the morning ration. The total is 57 pills and capsules every day. One of his chores before traveling to a meet is to place each of the three daily portions into an individual plastic bag. It is an amazing array. One suspects that Jenner pisses away enough vitamins and minerals to keep the average family of five fortified and healthy. Now, still wearing his sweatsuit, he sits in a plush armchair in the living room and thinks about the afternoon's agenda. He will throw the discus this afternoon. Yes, he has been neglecting the discus lately. And he will pole-vault, too, because he knows he could easily lose what he has worked so hard to gain in the pole vault. And his form in the hurdles has always disappointed him; of course he will run a few flights of hurdles.

The hurdles! He knows that he ought to run them better. He doesn't have great speed, but it is the technique that kills him. Somehow the technique has a way of slipping away from him just when he needs it most. His trailing leg gets all out of shape, or else his leading arm flaps up and down when it ought to be swinging hard and firm out in front of him like a left-handed boxer slamming an uppercut into his opponent's jaw. So he gets up from his plush chair, walks over to one corner of the room, and pulls into the center of the room a hurdle that is on a sort of permanent loan from the City College athletic department. Then he practices his form over the hurdle in slow motion, rising off his extended left leg, the right leg bent back with calf against thigh, clearing the way over the bar, and the left arm pulling through. A dozen times, two dozen times in slow motion over the hurdle. He is an optimist. Maybe, he thinks, maybe if he does it right often enough in the living room, he will do it right when he gets to Montreal.

Back to the plush chair now. He unrolls a long strip of photographs that show a Russian named Igor Ter-Ovanesyan making a 27-foot long jump. Jenner has been studying the photographs, and he thinks he has spotted something. It seems that Ter-Ovanesyan on this particular jump took a short, choppy, but powerful step before launching himself into the air. It is, Jenner thinks to himself, as though the Russian were gathering up all his accumulated speed and energy to expend in one furious burst at the point of takeoff. Jenner has been studying the photos for many days, and now he is convinced. A power step, he calls it. That makes sense. That is something for Jenner to try one of these days in training. Maybe he can find time for a few jumps today between the discus and the pole vault.

He finds the time. The technique feels strange but it has promise. He will try it again sometime soon. His vault feels good and so does the discus. He is taking turns in the discus cage—this time at San Jose State, a couple of miles from home—with Mac Wilkins. In the next few months, Wilkins will set a new world record in the event and win a gold medal. Jenner watches carefully when Wilkins throws. Jenner himself gets one out past 150 feet. He is capable of better, but that is still a long way to throw on a November afternoon with bad wind and the Games still eight months away.

He finishes his workout with a hard 440, once around the track. If he had a coach, this would probably be about the time that the coach would blow his whistle and pat Jenner on the back and congratulate him on a good, hard session. But Jenner hasn't had a coach since he left Graceland College. When he needs advice in specific events, he calls on friends like Wilkins and shot-putter Feuerbach. They are always happy to help. Jenner doesn't need anybody to pat him on the back at the end of a workout. He knows when he has done well. He also knows when he has not. When *The Decathlon*

Guide, a handbook of the sport, sent Jenner a questionnaire on his personal background and training regimen, Jenner listed one "Bertha Lou Jenner" as his coach. Bertha Lou Jenner is his golden Labrador retriever.

The San Jose YMCA is just a few minutes' drive from State. Jenner stops at his apartment long enough to shove his vaulting poles and their heavy cardboard containers behind the couch. Then he is off to the Y weight room. He cinches up a wide leather belt, pulls on a red tank top over his upper body. The top is a jersey that a Russian athlete gave him during Jenner's visit to Tallinn in 1974. It has a small black circle in the middle of the chest, and inside the circle, embroidered in gold metallic thread, is a laurel wreath that embraces a hammer and sickle. Jenner tells an onlooker that he wears the shirt simply because it is a good shirt. But maybe there is an element of shock value here that he enjoys, too.

The weight session runs one and a half hours, sometimes longer. He starts with five "reps"—repetitions—on the incline board. The board is slightly padded and covered in green vinyl. It is tilted at nearly 45 degrees and Jenner's legs are strapped to the top of the board. His job is to do sit-ups on this board, touching his elbows to his knees. And he does this while holding a weight against the back of his neck. He starts with a 25-pound weight and increases it by 10 and 15 pounds until he is doing it with 50 pounds held against the nape of his neck, the cold iron wrapped in a towel. Off the incline board, and more reps, sets of ten, with 90-pound barbells in each hand. He holds them at stomach level, palms facing upward, and pulls them up to shoulder height. Finally up to the lifting platform for a few tries with the big barbell. He shuffles the weights on the big bar, pulling some off and slapping others on, then fastens them in place with an adjustable collar at each end. He begins with 205 pounds. "Clean and jerk," lifters call this exercise. He yanks the bar off the platform and brings it up to chest level. It rests there for a moment, then two, three. Suddenly he shoves it overhead with an explosive move, sliding one foot forward and another back to duck under the weight of the bar, locking arms and then bringing the weight to full height by moving his feet back together again. He does this twice more at 230 pounds, three times at 250, twice more at 280. The strain shows in his face at these heavier weights. He grunts to get the bar off the platform. The muscles in his shoulders contort, show striations. He should quit now. But he still feels strong. . . . He will. Yes, he will go for the 310! A p.r. in the clean-and-jerk.

Fifteen more pounds on each end. His hands are sweaty; he rubs them in a box full of powdered chalk. He breathes deeply. The weight rises, not easily but surely, to his chest. That is the tough part. The jerk, one long breath later, is smooth and without pause. The arms lock, the bar wobbles and then holds firm. He brings it down to the floor and it bounces hard on the platform. Jenner grins as he unbuckles the leather belt.

"Awri-i-i-ight," he says under his breath.

Now, at nearly seven o'clock, the sky is dark when he parks outside his apartment building. He looks up toward the third floor, two windows across from the end. There is light behind the window and he can see his wife for a short moment as she walks behind the glass sliding doors that open out onto the small balcony. He is tired and hungry. He would like to stretch out on the heavy pile carpeting and nap before dinner. Instead he climbs up over the chain link fence and begins to run again.

Through the darkness he moves, alone with his thoughts and his reluctant body, and sometimes his dog. There is only a sliver of moon, so he runs in the dark, this time still in his full sweatsuit. Only one thing keeps him going now. Montreal, he reminds himself. The Games. The gold. After chasing the image for three years, the reality is close enough that he can imagine each step bringing him closer to the moment when he can reach out for it . . . grab the glory and hold . . . hold so tight that nobody can wrest it away from him. Like a brass ring on an old-fashioned merry-go-round. Time will bring it looming up in front of him, and for one instant it will be close enough that he can slip a finger around it. But for one instant, only one. Timing is the thing. He must be ready for that grasping lunge, because he will have only one chance before the brass ring is past him and gone forever.

The Games, he tells himself. The gold. It makes the laps go by more easily. He is alone on the track, and he likes it that way. It is a lonely job because there is nobody else to blame, nobody else to pick up part of the burden now and again when his arms and legs are weary, nobody else to do all the things that must be done. He is lonely now but he had better be used to the feeling, because he will be lonely out there on the floor of the stadium at Montreal—perhaps lonelier than ever.

Eighteen laps. Nineteen. Twenty. He doesn't stop running until he has reached the front door of the apartment. Then he flops on the floor of the living room and does stretching exercises until dinner. He sleeps well that night. It has not been an especially hard day, but it has been a good day. He drops off to sleep thinking about his new p.r. in the clean-and-jerk. Off the platfrom. Oooff! Over the head. Yes, a new p.r. Now time is running short. Spring will follow winter, after spring will come summer, and summer will bring the U.S. Trials and Montreal. It's nearly here. The days are dwindling. He wants all those days that remain to be at least as good as the one that has just passed.

He had always been serious about the decathlon. Now he was immersing himself in all of its subtleties and nuances. When he was not actually training, he was thinking about it. Though he was only vaguely aware of the mental exercise called psycho-cybernetics, he had adopted many of the principles of that process of visualization. And when he was not thinking about the decathlon, he was talking about it to almost anyone who would listen.

May 13, 1976

Every day I spend less and less time thinking about things other than the decathlon. When it gets to the last couple of weeks before the Games, it'll be 100 percent decathlon, no room for anything else. I couldn't get away from it now if I wanted to. I was invited today to talk to the students at Milpitas High School. What did I talk about? It sure wasn't English Lit. Then I went to a press conference, and people wanted to hear about the world record.

Other things don't really affect me. I can't get excited about anything but the decathlon. When I'm sitting around watching television, say, or eating dinner, I can't help thinking about it. Sometimes I think about getting into the starting blocks and getting a good jump on the gun. I think about the long jump at the Games. How far can I expect to go? How far are Dixon and Avilov and all the others going to jump, and how much are they going to gain on me? I think about the 400—the start, moving fast and relaxed down the backstretch, and then picking up the pace, accelerating through the turn. I've never been able to do that. I've never been strong enough. But that's the way I visualize myself doing it at Montreal, running away from all the rest of those guys when we come through the turn. That's how I want it to happen. I might run through a whole decathlon in my mind, over and over again every day. I think about each event and the things I have to do in order to score high. Then, when I'm actually in competition, I find myself doing those things naturally. That's why I have the hurdle here in the living room. Just walking through the motions here, looking at the hurdle and knowing what it feels like, all helps me run the hurdles better when I get into a race. Somehow I go out and run faster. What I see in my mind changes as I progress in the event.

99

Since I'm better at the hurdles than I used to be, I don't imagine myself doing the same things now that I did a year ago.

Sometimes I like to have a shot and a discus around to pick up and play with when I've got nothing better to do. I may pick up the shot, toss it up and down in the air, feel it, sometimes even sleep with it. I try to make friends with it, so that when it gets in my hand during a competition, it feels as though it belongs there. It's not a foreign object. It all gets back to the mind. The more I compete, the more convinced I am of the big part the mind plays in sports. Over the years, I've watched my mind and my body grow closer together. That's the way it ought to be, ideally, with no barrier between the two. When it's working right, your body should be able to go out and duplicate exactly what your mind imagines.

He never was bothered by the irony of his situation, the fact that he was amassing skills that would be useless to him after July 30. All the shot-putting expertise, the speed and power, would be only arcane abilities after the decathlon. He had decided several years earlier that the decathlon at Montreal would be his last. He would be overdue to take up residence again in the real world. That was the last and most crucial aspect of the mental contract he had drawn up with himself after Munich. There would be no second chances.

May 18, 1976

I love the training. I love the hard work and the competition. I don't think I'll find it easy to quit. But that's the way it has to be. Otherwise, when I get tired or the competition gets tough and I'm in a tight spot, it would be too easy to say, "Oh well, forget it. I'll do it next time."

When I was a competitive water-skier, I never imagined myself ever leaving it. I saw myself skiing forever. I couldn't see why I would ever want to stop, because I

*enjoyed it and I kept getting better at it. If someone had
told me back in 1968 that in a couple of years I would never
ski again, I'd have said he was crazy. But I did leave it,
because I found something else.*

*My situation now is a little different. I don't have any-
thing else after the Olympics. I haven't had the time or the
inclination to think about what I'll do July 31. People talk
to me about television, sportscasting, the movies, but I
don't want to hear about it now.*

*There's another factor that never bothered me before. I
can see the day coming when I won't be as fast and as
strong as I am now. I want to quit before that happens. I
don't want to keep hanging on. I keep thinking about what
a great athlete Johnny Unitas was, and how he kept on
playing even after he couldn't do the same things he used to
do easily. I don't want that to happen. It's a matter of
pride. If people are going to remember me, I want them to
have an image of me when I was at my best. I don't want to
spoil it. That means that when I walk off the field at
Montreal, I'm literally not going to look back. I'll say to
myself, "Fine, that was fun, but now it's time for something
else." If I win the gold medal, there won't be anything else
for me in the decathlon, anyway. I've already got the world
record, and a second medal can't possibly mean as much as
the first. And if I should lose, then I'll just tell myself that I
gave it my best shot, did everything I possibly could, and
that for two days another guy was better than I was. Losing
will make it harder to quit, but I'm quitting anyway. I've
got to draw the line.*

One night that spring they were invited to a celebrity party in
Hollywood, courtesy of a national magazine which had lately
made the Jenners almost a weekly feature of its pages. He
returned and talked more reflectively than usual about the
consequences of a victory at Montreal. It was a subject that he
generally dismissed; there would be time to consider that

later, he would say. But it was about this time that he was approached by an aide to movie producer Ilya Salkind, who had begun casting *Superman* and needed someone for the title role.

May 18, 1976

The party was interesting. It exposed me to people and a way of life that I've never seen before. We met Henry Winkler, who plays the character called Fonzie on a TV comedy series. Very nice, very polite, and not at all like the character he plays in the show. Chrystie got a kick out of meeting him and so did I. We tried to be cool about it. That made me think later, on the plane coming back. I'm not sure that Chrystie and I are ready for being famous and all that it entails. Poor Henry Winkler is so well known that there's no way he can walk to the grocery store without attracting attention. No way he can have a quiet dinner in a restaurant and then go to a movie. That means you end up spending all your time with people who are just as famous and visible as you are, because they're the only ones who won't make a fuss over you.

At the moment, I get a kick out of people stopping me on the street and asking me for an autograph. But I'm not so well known that it happens all the time. It could get tiresome after a couple of years. All this is strange to me, because I'm still the same person I always was. I'm a guy who runs and jumps. The only difference is that now I'm scoring more points, and all of a sudden, for that reason, people are paying attention to me. I'm the same inside, but the way people react to me has changed.

I don't know too much about the Superman thing, except that it's the title role and there will be a lot of really big people involved. I've heard Marlon Brando, Gene Hackman mentioned. Heck of a way to start acting, if it happens. We'll see about it after the Games. It set me back for a while, thinking that it could happen. Chrystie got a very strange look in her eye when I told her about it. It was a kind of disbelief: "This husband of mine, the guy I found going to school in Iowa, might turn out to be a movie star." She wasn't overjoyed by any means.

I could understand if she did have mixed feelings about it. We had a very happy life together before any of this happened, when I was just another decathlete trying to score 8,000 points. Now there's a possibility that it could all change, change really quickly, and that can be hard to take. Sometimes it's hard for me to grasp what I've done and what I could be getting myself into.

Whatever comes of it, if I win the gold, I don't want it to be a pure money-making scheme. I'm not dumb. I'd like to make enough money so that I can live the way I want and never have to worry about it again, but I don't want to grab the bread and run the way some jocks have done. I'd like to make the world a little better somehow. I don't expect that I can turn the world around; but I'm not such a cynic, either, that I think no single person can make a difference. The man who wins the gold medal in the decathlon has some power, some influence. People admire him. When he has something to say, they'll listen to him, as long as he doesn't abuse the privilege. You can sell out, you can waste it, or you can try to use it for some good.

(Soon after he had won the gold medal, Jenner flew to Rome for a screen test for the role of Superman. Wearing ski clothes and a cape, which were supposed to simulate the comic book hero's costume, and with his hair slicked by a generous application of mineral oil, Jenner played out a scene of the movie before cameras in the Cinecitta studio. Though he got kind words from director Guy Hamilton, Jenner did not get the part. The role called for a character near 40 years old. Jenner, with his unlined face and his healthy tan, did not photograph any older than his 26 years.)

His life fell into a monotonous rhythm that winter. And that made him very happy. He feared more than anything the chance of injury that could keep him off the training field and interrupt his progress.

November 11, 1975

It could happen anytime. It scares you to think about it but that's part of the life. I take care of my body, but these things happen, sometimes.

Many decathletes spend the major part of their careers nursing injuries. It is, as Jenner says, one of the hazards of the profession. Every day of training is also a day of stress, and sometimes the body gives in to the stress. Weight training builds strength, but the new muscles are also susceptible to pulls and strains.

With a half hour of stretching exercises every morning, Jenner had been able to run hard every day without aggravating his sore Achilles tendon. He tended and pampered his body in a nervous fashion that would have been narcissistic if it had not been so necessary for success.

May 1, 1976

After a while you get to know your body and to understand it. You learn what's a bad injury and what's a good injury—an injury that you can live with. You learn to feel pulls and strains before they happen. And the older I get, the better I am at that kind of thing.

Take a hamstring pull. I know the feeling. I can feel it coming. I can tell whether it's just sore from a hard workout the day before or whether it's ready to go. And when I feel it going, then I don't run for a day or so. I've avoided an injury. It costs me one or two days of training, but it could have meant a month otherwise.

Now I know, for example, that I've got to be doubly

careful when I run the day after a hard workout. If I want to do something explosive, such as the high jump, then I've got to get loose, warm up extra well. If I jump right into it as though I were fresh and rested, something's going to go. When I was younger, I would think nothing of a little pain in my leg. And then I'd be out two weeks waiting for it to heal because I had run on it when I shouldn't have. But I can't afford that now. Especially now. Two weeks is a long time now. Two weeks could be a career now.

Jenner entered the Drake Relays that spring. The meet, the last weekend in April, would be his first competition of the year. He was anxious to test himself again, and he had always enjoyed Drake because it gave him an excuse to visit Iowa and see old school friends again. He had, after all, run his first decathlon here and it gave him some satisfaction to return as world-record holder.

But he did not take the meet so seriously that he relaxed his winter training schedule. He worked out until the morning that he and Chrystie flew to Des Moines. The day before he left, he was practicing his technique in the shot put.

I was throwing a light shot, just 14½ pounds, not worrying about distance. I was working on my lower body, which is so important in the shot, and I wasn't paying enough attention to what my arm was doing. My arm got out of whack on a throw and the shot pulled my finger back. It started to hurt right away and I knew that I'd wrenched a tendon in the hand. I didn't need a doctor to tell me that. I put it on ice and it started hurting more. This was four days before I was supposed to compete at Drake. The first three days, I couldn't even hold the shot. I felt lucky when I threw it 45 feet the next day in the meet.

That tendon is crucial to the shot put. The iron ball rests at the base of the fingers, and a flip of the wrist gives the shot its final shove as the body reaches full extension and the throwing arm straightens. That last flick of the hand is the difference between a good throw and a mediocre one. With the injured tendon, the entire throw became painful, since all the force generated by the legs, the torso, and the arm is channeled through that narrow ridge at the base of the fingers. Since his grip was not weakened, none of the other events was affected. But putting the shot was impossible. Rest was the only cure. He would lose weeks of practice with the shot and there still was no guarantee that the hand would be healthy for the Games.

Even with his poor put, he scored 8,250 and won Drake for the third time. That would be his last decathlon until the Olympic Trials in June, at Eugene. He refused an invitation to run May 15 and 16 at a meet in Gotzis, Austria. So he missed one of the more remarkable decathlon competitions in recent years.

The winner by 51 points was a 22-year-old West German named Guido Kratschmer, who scored 250 points over his previous p.r. with a total of 8,381, fourth-highest score in history and a new national record. Nobody had ever scored so many points and still failed to set a world record. In second place was an Austrian named Sepp Zeilbauer. His total of 8,310 could have been good for fifth place on the all-time list. But that same day, a Russian named Aleksander Grebeniuk had scored 8,330 in a meet at Sochi, USSR, for "B" team decathletes, essentially second-stringers.

Jenner got news of these scores via a phone call from a friendly staff writer at *Track & Field News,* the sport's top periodical in this country. This was also how he heard of Avilov's 8,336 in a meet several weeks before the Trials, the Russian's highest total since Munich. He heard, too, of an 8,280 score by East German Seigfried Stark, one of 8,249 by Litvinenko, another of 8,119 by West German Eberhard Stroot.

Jenner was not surprised. This was an Olympic year. He

wasn't the only one who had been working hard over the winter. He seemed unconcerned that his 8,250 at Drake was only the sixth-highest score of the season as he went into the Trials. Besides, he had other problems.

Instead of running in Austria, he had decided to enter an all-comer's meet in Santa Barbara. He would compete in the discus, the pole vault, and the 400 meters. It would be just another workout. He and Chrystie had bought camping gear and planned to camp out at one of the nearby state beaches.

The workout/camping trip nearly cost him the gold. He had been jumping poorly, slowing as he approached the pit instead of accelerating. He cleared the bar at 15 feet but fell awkwardly. His upper body and his arms hit the thickly padded foam cushion, but his legs hit the runway and one knee struck the wooden box. He jumped once more, before the knee—the same knee that had been injured when he was at Graceland—began to swell. He was unable to bend his leg that night. But three days later he was back on the track and set a p.r. in his 220-yard sprint workouts. He ran another meet two weeks later at Laney College, this time finishing second in an open half-mile race in one minute, 55 seconds, and throwing the discus 174 feet, 11 inches, a new p.r. If that throw had come in a decathlon competition, it would have qualified as the longest throw ever by a decathlete.

June 1, 1976

Something like that, it does me good. I need competition, even if it is just an all-comer's meet, because when you train day after day it's difficult to give the best you've got. But competition draws it out of you, if you've got it in the first place.

It's so easy to start doubting your own abilities. I hadn't thrown the discus in competition for a while, and I started thinking that 165 feet is a long way to throw. I start to wonder, maybe I couldn't do it again if I had to. So I needed the competition to keep up my faith in myself.

Each Olympic year, *Track & Field News* publishes predictions on the outcome of each event in both the U.S. Trials and the Games. The magazine containing the predictions for 1976 arrived June 10 in the Jenner household. The editors had picked Jenner to win both the Trials and the Olympics. Jenner read the issue one morning as he was scalding the underside of his right thigh with a heating pad. He was treating a pulled hamstring muscle, probably his most serious injury since his back problems in 1973. And it had come just three weeks before he was to compete at the Trials in Eugene. That was his only way of getting to Montreal, and if he failed at Eugene to place among the top three scorers—for any reason—then he could not compete in the Olympics. The U.S. Olympic Committee made no exceptions, even in the case of world-record holders with pulled hamstrings.

He was subdued but far from maudlin when he spoke with me that morning. He described how the muscle had been pulled. There was, he admitted, a chance that the muscle would not heal quickly enough for him to be competitive at Eugene. It could affect every one of the ten events. And that would be the end, he would not see Montreal.

After he had sat for five minutes on the heating pad, he used a metal spoon to rub several drops of a clear, colorless liquid into the skin above the hamstring. The liquid was DMSO (an acronym for a polysyllabic chemical compound derived from wood pulp), often seen in racetrack barns. Though it is still experimental in the treatment of humans, its heavy, pungent smell is a common feature of professional football locker rooms. Team physicians prize the substance for its unique property of penetrating muscle tissue completely and almost instantly. They often use it with other medications—to carry cortisone into joints and deep muscle masses, for example. Even used alone, it helps to relieve muscle pulls and strains, though nobody is sure why this is so. Not that Jenner cared. It worked, and that was enough.

108

June 10, 1976

It was a freak thing. I was jogging out on the edge of the track and my foot came down wrong. It twisted around kind of funny. And that was it. I felt it go. I know I brag about being able to feel a hamstring getting ready to go, but this one didn't give me any warning. The first 48 hours I put ice on it. Then heat. I take a heating pad, put it in boiling water, then I let it burn the heck out of my leg. Then I alternate heat and ice, every five minutes; that gets the circulation going, which is what I need down there. Then I get a rubdown and use DMSO. I wish I could get my hands on some cortisone, too. Oh, yes, and you eat a lot of bananas. Bananas are high in potassium, which helps to promote healing of muscles. That's really true. And then you hope it gets better very soon.

Before I start feeling sorry for myself, I think that I'm not the only guy who's hurting. I hear Dixon has got a really bad elbow on his throwing arm. I've seen some of his workout times. He's been flying, just flying, but I hear he can't throw the javelin at all. I notice **Track & Field News** *didn't pick him to finish in the top three at the Trials. Maybe the elbow is as bad as everybody says. But he'll have lots of points the first day, and he's talented enough that I'll bet he gets the javelin out there 150 feet even if it kills him.*

Funny thing about those predictions. Those guys haven't been right the last two times. I don't know who they picked in 1964, but they picked Bendlin to beat Toomey in 1968 and they picked Bannister to beat Avilov in 1972. So now they pick Jenner in 1976. It doesn't affect me one way or the other, if you want to know the truth. Somebody's prediction won't win it for me or lose it for me. I don't let that stuff influence me. I like to think that my destiny is in my own hands. Sure, I know there's no way of getting around unavoidable injuries, but I feel I'm the only one who's responsible for what I do on the field.

Chrystie got interested in biorhythm recently. Every-
body is supposed to go through cycles, highs and lows, in
their physical, mental, and emotional states. Some days
you're high and some days you're low, depending on your
birth date. I didn't want to hear about it when she brought
it up. Suppose I find out that I'm on a triple low on July 29
and 30. Then what am I supposed to do? Give up and tell
Avilov that he can have the gold medal? I'm much better off
if I regard all that stuff as a lot of b.s., at least until all this
is over.

The trial meet for selection of the U.S. track and field team
began June 19 in Eugene, Oregon. At first Jenner planned to
arrive in Eugene only a day or two before the decathlon was
to begin, on June 25. But he is a track fan, with many friends
in the sport. So while Chrystie flew what was to be her last
assignment with United Airlines, Bruce flew to Eugene,
checked into his dormitory room, and watched the competition every day from the stands and from the side of the track.
He kept a running total of the number of San Jose athletes to
qualify for the team. (Including Jenner, the number would be
11.)

When he left for Eugene, six weeks remained before the
Olympic decathlon. These were the last six weeks of his
athletic life, and also the most significant.

June 15, 1976

It's an unusual situation in some respects. I get all caught
up in how important the next month and a half will be, but
I'm constantly reminded that I'm coming to the end of a big
part of my life. When I go out and throw the discus, I can't
help thinking, "Hey, you're not going to be doing this too
much longer." All the work is over now. The only thing left
is the performing.

Win or lose, I'm glad I did it. If things don't turn out the

110

way I want, I'll accept that. It won't change anything. The reason is that I enjoyed what I was doing. All the hard work and the sacrifice, I did that because I wanted to do it. I'm no martyr. I love running and jumping and throwing.

If I win the gold medal, it'll be easy to say, "Yes, it was all worth it." If I don't, the answer will be the same. It was all worth it. I wouldn't have wanted it any different.

Maybe that explains why, even during the low points in the last few years, I never gave it up. Even at Penn State when I looked so bad, back in 1973, even when I screwed up in Santa Barbara in 1975, I stayed with it. It was too important to my life to give it up then. I loved what I was doing. I still love it.

**Eugene and
the Trials**

Eugene, Oregon
June 25, 1976
11:00 A.M.

When last call comes over the loudspeakers for the 100-meter decathlon dash, Jenner is high-stepping down the track, legs pumping, knees rising chest-high and then slamming down to the hard rubberish synthetic-surfaced track. He chatters off 50 yards of steps that way before he stops, turns, walks back to the starting line. His hands are on his hips. He breathes slowly, deliberately, fully. He looks like a man ready to throw the first punch in a bar fight. There are seven other decathletes in this first heat. Some of them are standing behind the starting blocks, shaking their legs to loosen the muscles. Others prance down the track, their legs flashing. But none seems quite so ready to run as Jenner.

Racehorses are that way. Their trainers call them dumb animals, but the horses know when they are going to race. Some of them balk at the starting gate; they must be coaxed and sometimes pushed into place. But others trot in willingly, arching their necks in anticipation and pawing the ground. And that is the image that comes to mind as I watch

Jenner. He is ready. His nostrils flare as he chuffs in a lungful of air. The morning is cool, and Jenner is wearing deep blue sweatpants and a light blue T-shirt with a message printed across the front. The message reads: "FEET DON'T FAIL ME NOW."

There are sixteen decathletes here, trying for the three spots on the U.S. team. The 100-meter sprint is broken down into two heats, eight runners per heat, with heat and lane assignments drawn by lot before the race. Jenner has drawn heat one, lane one, closest to the infield. Dixon, Fred Samara, and Jeff Bennett, the best sprinters of these sixteen, all will run in the second heat. That shouldn't matter, since each man is running against the clock and the tables, but I know from talking to Jenner that he likes to chase a faster man.

The sweatpants and the T-shirt come off and Jenner crouches down in the aluminum starting blocks. Off the track to Jenner's left, kneeling on one leg, is the starter. He raises his right arm, with a pistol in his hand.

Bob Coffman, running in lane seven, jumps the gun the first time the runners settle into the blocks. Tony Hale, a strong but inexperienced decathlete from Fisk University, jumps out before the gun the second time. The third try is good. Good for everybody but Jenner. His first two strides out of the blocks are strong and sure, but he seems to land awkwardly on the third or fourth. It is not so much a stumble as a subtle break in rhythm. But it is enough to put him behind the rest of the field. His arms flail the air, furiously. His legs pump, shoes slapping a frantic beat against the Tartan surface. But he is accelerating. He loses no more ground. And in the last 30 yards he may be the fastest man on the track. Coffman wins by a tenth of a second, timed by stopwatches at 10.6. Rex Harvey, running closest to Jenner in lane two, is second. But Jenner makes up the gap between himself and Harvey and the two are shoulder to shoulder at the finish. Both are timed at 10.7, worth 879 points. The time equals Jenner's personal record in the event.

Jenner pulls on the T-shirt and the sweatpants again. He saunters over to a small metal shed at one corner of MacArthur Field. He is sitting in a metal folding chair when the first-heat times are announced.

"I could go for the record," Jenner says. He smiles.

That puts everything into a most realistic perspective. If Jenner is competing against anyone here, it is against himself, the athlete he was those two days on this same track in August. That is his closest competition. If he can stay close to that score, he will win his spot on the team. Nobody else will be close. And his pursuit is made easier when the electronic timing system fails in the second heat and the meet officials must score the race with times taken from stopwatches.

It is not a negligible point. A human timer, hearing the report of a starter's pistol, does not react instantly. The sound of the pistol must register in the mind; the message to jab the starting button on the stopwatch must course neurons and leap synapses before the muscles of the thumb can contract. The automatic timer begins registering the milliseconds as soon as the trigger is pulled on the starter's gun, whereas the human timer needs as much as two-tenths of a second to set his mechanical timepiece in motion. Two-tenths of a second means 52 points in the 100 meters, more than 20 points in the hurdles.

The difference is great enough that to use electronic scores in one heat and the hand-timed version in another would be unfair, officials decide. So hand-timed scores are announced for both heats. Jenner was caught by the electronic clocks at 10.93—still one of his best 100-meter races ever—but 10.7 was announced and recorded. There would be more of that later.

I was just glad that it was over. When I got across the finish line, I yelled out "All right! We got this thing going." The waiting is so tough. You can't work the week before a decathlon, because you've got to conserve your energy. So

117

you've got all this energy building up inside you and noth-
ing to do with it. You've got no release. The wait goes on
and on. And on top of it all, I was thinking about my
hamstring, wondering how it would feel. I knew that if I
had a good race, got a good time, I'd be on my way. And I
did. A little stumble, but really strong at the end. It was
such a relief finally to get the thing started.

Fred Samara gets 932 points for his 10.5 in winning the second heat. Dixon and Coffman have 905 each. Jenner ties Harvey and Jeff Bennett with 879.

Noon

Jenner says Eugene is his favorite place for a track meet. If he had qualified for the Olympic team and set a world record at Death Valley, then he would call Death Valley his favorite place for a track meet. Whatever his reasons, he's got a point. There probably isn't a more track-crazy, health-conscious city in America. What Los Angeles is to automobiles, free-ways, and smog, Eugene is to bicycles, jogging trails, and crisp air. All these reasons make Eugene an ideal place to choose the nation's Olympic track and field team. Steve Prefontaine became one of the world's top distance runners running for the University of Oregon here. He stayed in Eugene after leaving school and he was probably the most important man in town until the night he died—in an au-tomobile accident, after running a 5000-meter race at MacAr-thur Field. The streets, sidewalks, and parks are full of run-ners in the morning and the evening and the hours in be-tween. One of the most popular spots in town is a jogging trail near the university campus. The trail is named for Prefon-taine, and it meanders several miles through parkland near the Willamette River where Prefontaine used to train. The hills around the town are lush and green, just the way hills in west-central Oregon are supposed to be. The air is clean, and

Bruce stretches to win, but comes in second in the 1,500-meter event to Argentina's
Tito Steiner at the Pan Am Games in Mexico City, October 1975. Bruce set a Pan
Am Game record, winning the Decathlon with 8,045 points.

On the first day of the Decathlon, Bruce clears the bar 6 feet 8 inches on his third try in the High Jump. (Heinz Kluetmeier for Sports Illustrated)

Gutting out the final strides—the last split seconds in the 400-meter run. He ran a personal best of 47.5 seconds in this last event of the first day. (James Drake for Sports Illustrated)

Chrystie watches in dismay as Bruce misses his first attempt at 4.70 meters in the Pole Vault. To her left is Bruce's mother, Esther. (Wide World Photo)

sometimes when the wind is right it carries a faint fresh sawdust scent from the mills on the outskirts of town.

For other reasons, the wind has been important all week to officials and competitors here. It can be crucial in the javelin and the discus. And if a world record is to be set in a running, jumping, or throwing event, then the wind must not exceed the maximum set by the International Amateur Athletic Federation, arbiter of such matters. In the decathlon, the limit is 4 meters per second, or about 9 miles per hour.

The wind rises, gusts, dies, and rises capriciously as the decathletes begin their first rounds in the long jump. They sprint down a runway and leap into a smooth, sandy pit. The athletes take three jumps, one at a time, in an order that has been determined by draw. Jenner jumps fourth in the first round, then sits on the grass near the jumping pit to wait his turn in the second round.

His first jump is a poor one, measuring 23 feet, three-quarters of an inch. That is almost a foot short of his lifetime best mark in the event. His second jump is much better: 23-8. But at the moment he jumps, the wind gusts at his back and the anemometer near the runway registers 4.3 meters per second. It doesn't nullify the jump, but the mark can't count toward any world record. His third try, a few minutes later, may be his best. He grunts heavily as he throws his body forward. His arms thrust forward as he falls into the sand. But his body rocks backward slightly and the closest mark to the foul line is a dished-out impression left by his butt as he fought to regain his balance. Still, the jump measures 23-7 and the wind is legal.

Jeff Bennett is the third jumper, behind Jenner. His first two jumps are barely over 23 feet. For his third attempt, his takeoff is awkward. He falls short and cries out when his body hits the sand. He writhes there for several seconds before somebody realizes that he is not just agonizing over a poor jump. A doctor comes running, bends over Bennett in the pit while Bennett lies there, his face stretched with pain. Then he is pulled up from the sand. There is a big man at each shoulder to help him across the track to the trainers' tent. He hops on his left leg while his right dangles free. Jenner watches this for a few seconds and then looks elsewhere.

"A hamstring," Jenner tells me. "He knew it was going, too. He said so after his second jump."

And so Bennett is out. It is a sobering absence. Other decathletes respected Bennett, for between Bill Toomey's retirement in 1969 and Jenner's emergence as an international star four years later, Bennett was one of this country's few world-class decathletes. He was a contender for a medal at Munich, but Avilov's brilliant performance, and a fall during the hurdles when he was jostled by the eventual bronze medalist, shoved Bennett to fourth place, 10 points short of a medal. At 5-8, 152 pounds, he was the smallest of the very good decathletes. And Jenner remembers being awed at his style and power in winning the Drake Relays of 1970, Jenner's first decathlon.

And now he is finished. A hamstring. If nobody seems to want to talk about it, perhaps that is because they all know it is exactly the sort of thing that could happen to any one of them.

Bill Hancock, a superb jumper from the University of Chicago Track Club, wins the long jump at 25-5½. Dixon is second at 24-10½, with 937 points, to take the overall lead. Jenner's 879 points put him in sixth place. But it also puts him ahead of the pace which he set in August.

1:20 P.M.

Jenner is in the stands, sitting with Chrystie, friends, his mother. Everybody except Jenner is wearing yellow T-shirts that say "GO JENNER GO" on the back. The first round of the shot put is 40 minutes away. Jenner is smiling. He has been doing a lot of that so far.

"I couldn't believe it," he says. "I actually slept last night. I was tossing and turning the way I always do before a big meet, and the clock said ten thirty. The next thing I knew, the clock said six thirty. And then I went back to sleep for another hour. I've been up here for a week, sitting and staring at the walls. Maybe I came up too early but all my San Jose buddies were up here qualifying and I had to watch."

"Shot put next," I say. "What are you trying to get out of the shot put?"

The smile disappears. He holds up his left hand and wiggles his fingers. A dumb question.

"Anything I can get," he says.

2:00 P.M.

Jenner shakes his left hand, shakes it again, picks up the round, iron, 16-pound ball in his left hand. He hefts it, turns his back to the throwing area, crouches, and tilts his head until the shot rests against the hinge of his jaw on his left side. He whirls in the throwing circle, his weight low. His left arm straightens, the shot arches away and falls 45 feet, 11½ inches away.

That first throw is at least 3 feet short of what Jenner would consider a good mark. His second is hardly longer, 46-0¾. His third is the shortest of all, 44-5. But his second put is still the fourth longest of the day, and his 731 points send him to fourth place overall behind Dixon—who wins the shot at 48-7—Coffman, and Samara. But in August, Jenner had putted a lifetime best, over 50 feet. So now he trails by 74 points the only athlete he's really chasing this weekend.

July 2, 1976

My hand bothers the heck out of me. It bothered me in the Trials, and it'll bother me right through the Games. I'm going to be throwing short and I can't help it. I even tried throwing right-handed in practice. It didn't work. But I tried.

From the time that Rex Harvey sails over the bar at 5-feet-7 until Bill Hancock knocks that same bar sailing with his leg on his third try at 7-2¼, there are 133 attempts in the high jump, at seventeen different heights, with an average of nearly a minute elapsing between each jump. But Jenner plays the waiting game well. He passes at the first two low heights, clears easily on his first jump at 6-0½, passes again, and then clears 6-3¼. He passes at 6-4½ and clears 6-5½ while the crowd of nearly 15,000 people applauds the finishers in a 5000 meter qualifying run. (The decathlon doesn't have the stadium to itself; track meets could have been prototypes for the first three-ring circus. While the decathletes were running the 100-meter heats in the morning, the men's triple-jump specialists were leaping into the sand pit. When the decathletes took over in the jumping area, the women 1500-meter runners were beginning their qualifying heats.)

Jenner misses for the first time with the bar at 6-6¾. His body clears the barrier but a leg brushes it enough to knock the bar off its perch on the upright standards. But on his second try, he is over without trouble. The jump is worth 857 points, and it puts him at least temporarily into second place. Dixon has cleared his first jump at 6-6¾. Both Jenner and Dixon miss their three tries at the next height, 6-8, and Bill Hancock pushes Jenner to third when he equals the U.S. decathlon high jump record by soaring over the bar on his second try at 7-1½. That is good for an even 1,000 points.

In August, Jenner had cleared 6-7½ here. But officials bypass that height this time in advancing the bar in increments of three centimeters, about 1¼ inches.

Jenner is close each time to clearing 6-8.

"I'll do it in Montreal," he says after he misses the third time. "I couldn't really concentrate on it this time, but I will in Montreal. So I'm saving that one for the Games. Hey, I've got to have something to keep reaching for, you know."

6:17 P.M.

Jenner comes walking away from the draw for the 400-meter heat assignments. He is smiling again.

"I got Dixon in my heat," he says. "And right beside me, too."

6:56 P.M.

Jenner is in the last of three heats, starting on the outermost lane, with Dixon nearest to him on the left. The starting blocks are staggered, since a complete circuit of the track running in the outside lane measures approximately 45 feet more than the 440 yards of the inside lane. So Jenner, starting in the outermost lane, will have an initial lead that ought to disappear as the runners on the inside begin making up ground by running a shorter distance through the turns. For that reason, it's difficult to gauge the progress of the 400 meters until the runners come off the last turn and head down the straight.

Predictably, Jenner takes the lead going into the back straight. The breeze that was such a factor in the long jump is now in the runners' faces as they pound down the stretch. And now the wind seems even heavier. The strain shows on Jenner's face. He holds his lead halfway through the last turn. Steadily, Dixon erases it by running the slightly shorter distance through the turn until he is at Jenner's left shoulder. For three, four strides, they are shoulder to shoulder.

And then Jenner begins to pull away. His strides are longer, faster, stronger. This late in the day, the decathletes are alone on the stadium floor, no other distractions for the crowd. They know track, these people in Eugene. They know that Jenner on the outside lane is not supposed to run away from Dixon on the inside. And so they cheer, loudly, as the runners empty onto the front straight and head for the tape.

Dixon makes up some distance, but not enough. Jenner breasts the tape in 48.7, a tenth of a second faster than Dixon.

It is also the fastest time in all of the three heats of the 400 meters, worth 866 points, which put him at 4,196 at the end of the first day. He is 54 points short of Hancock, 141 behind Dixon in first place, and 72 points behind his own record pace.

Jenner comes trotting through the first turn, his chest heaving every couple of seconds, sweat showing on his shoulders and along his brow. I reach out for his hand; his grip is strong and sure. But he seems not to recognize me. His face is contorted strangely. Part of it, I know, is from the pain of sprinting nearly a quarter-mile. But there is something else I haven't seen there before, a leering, triumphant, wolfish glare that he seems to be directing at the rest of the world.

And then it is gone. Smiling, too-nice, straight and even teeth, Jenner is back where he belongs. He jogs around the track with a coterie of kids following. He stops every few feet to sign an autograph. "Warming down," he calls this.

When he has finished jogging, he signs autographs. He walks over to the metal shed to answer questions from reporters. (Yes, he thinks he's in good shape, sitting third already with his strong second day still to come. No, he doesn't think he has much of a shot at the world record.)

He is walking down the track to see Chrystie when a man who says he is a physician stops him. The man wants to know about training and nutrition. Bruce talks to him politely for a few minutes, makes dinner plans with Chrystie—a researcher from *Sports Illustrated* will be with them—and then we walk out of the stadium toward his dormitory room across the street.

He does stretching exercises on the floor of his room while we talk. He is running well, he says, as well as he ever has. He wishes there hadn't been the foul-up with the automatic timing in the 100. He *might* have a shot at the record, he says. If he could throw the discus 175 feet, pole-vault over 16, throw the javelin 220 or so . . .

"That damn shot put," he says. He wiggles the finger of his left hand again.

The hurdles race that begins tomorrow's competition will be crucial, he tells me. If he scores well there, then he may yet have a chance at raising the record.

"What the heck," he says. "Why not? You don't get a chance to set a world's record every day."

Then he mentions, in an offhand way, that today is the first time he has ever beaten Dixon in the 400 meters.

I remember that flash of out-of-character arrogance on his face at the end of the race. And now I understand it.

June 26, 1976

10:00 A.M.

The officials have decided to start the thirteen remaining decathletes (Bennett and two others having been scratched because of injury or illness) in four heats, with at least one lane separating each runner, to eliminate the jostling that can occur as the runners clear each set of hurdles.

Jenner is in the third heat. He watches Samara run second to Mike Hill in the first heat and sees Dixon win the second heat in 14.82. Jenner is running with Steve Gough and Bill Hancock, both of whom have p.r.'s at least two-tenths of a second faster than Jenner's. But he breaks out of the blocks smoothly, stays even with Gough and Hancock through the first four sets of hurdles, and then opens up a half-step lead as they leave the last hurdles behind them and dash for the finish. His time, caught by the electronic clock, is 14.57 seconds. It is by far the greatest hurdles race of his life, faster even than his hand-timed mark of 14.6 set here in August.

So Dixon still leads, but his margin has shrunk where he had expected to pad it. He has 5,205. Hancock is second, with 5,114. Jenner has 5,092, still 68 points behind his own pace. The automatic timing has cost him 22 points.

11:00 A.M.

The flag whips and slaps in the breezes at one end of the stadium, then collapses, then unfurls and snaps. The wind's strength and direction are important to the decathletes as they begin to throw the discus now. Sometimes it is a good, quartering wind. But just as often it is an unfavorable wind or no wind at all.

Jenner is lucky when he throws the first time. The breeze is strong enough to ruffle the flag and it wafts in from Jenner's left side as he releases the discus—the ideal lefty's wind. The discus carries, carries. The trajectory is higher than he would like, but when the discus smacks into the earth, cutting a divot, it falls less than a foot short of Rafer Johnson's U.S. decathlon discus record, marked by a white ribbon stretched across the throwing sector. A measuring tape is stretched out from the edge of the throwing circle to the scar in the earth. The mark is 169 feet, 7 inches. The first throw stands. He fouls on the second try while throwing 160 feet, and he gets the discus out only 156 feet on his third attempt, this time against the wind. But 169-7 is his decathlon p.r. It is worth 901 points, the most he has ever scored in this event. It is 30 points more than he scored in August.

Gough is second with a throw of 166-7. Dixon fouls his first throw; is careful to make a legal attempt the second time, throwing only 145-10; and finally throws close to his potential the third time: 152-11, and is credited with 811 points. Hancock throws 138-5 and slips out of contention. So now Jenner is in second place, 22 points behind Dixon.

3:18 P.M.

It is about this point that Jenner was to catch Dixon and disappear. But Dixon isn't getting caught and that is partly because Jenner doesn't seem especially anxious to do any chasing.

Dixon is supposed to be a poor vaulter. His p.r. in the

126

event—until this afternoon—was 13-9. Almost *everybody* vaults higher than Dixon. So great is the difference between Jenner and Dixon in this event that Dixon is usually out of the competition before Jenner flies over the bar at his opening height.

This time Dixon clears the bar on his first try at 13-5½. He passes at his p.r. height of 13-9½, then calmly clears again on his first try at 14-1¼. And Jenner misses his first try at that height, hitting the bar with his foot while he is still on his way up. He clears easily the second time, and goes to sit on the grass nearby. But he is watching Dixon a lot more closely then he usually does in the pole vault. Now, at 14-5, Dixon again clears on his first attempt. He misses badly the first two times at 14-9½—a full foot higher than he has ever before vaulted in competition—but the third time he snakes over without disturbing the bar.

Jenner has passed at these last two heights. He jumps at 15-1¼ and goes over. So does Dixon, again on his first attempt. Now the bar goes to 15-5. It must look impossibly tough to Dixon. And this time, he misses all three attempts. But his new p.r. of 15-1¼ has been good for 957 points and a total of 7,973.

Jenner has passed at 15-5. He is thinking about 16 feet, but decides to try 15-9 first. Now only he and Craig Brigham are still jumping. Brigham clears 15-9 his first time over. Jenner has enough height on his first try but brushes the bar with a foot on the way up. The standards can be moved back and forth over the planting box as much as 2 feet, and Jenner asks that they be moved back as far as possible before he jumps the second time. But he simply lacks the height on this attempt and the skinny bar goes flying off its perch.

Before he jumps a third time, he rests the grip end of the pole in a notched stake near the runway. He walks up to the standards, checks the alignment, then retrieves his pole and makes one practice approach down the runway. Then he is ready. He tightens his grip on the pole, points the long shaft down the runway, rocks backward, and then begins his approach. His legs pump high. His speed, his approach, are good. He plants the tip, the pole bends, and then whips up off the ground, into the sky. He is high enough to clear 16 feet, maybe even 16-6. And he has still not reached the apex of his jump when one foot brushes against the bar and knocks it to the ground.

His last successful jump was at 15-1¼. So he ties with Dixon and is still in second place. In August, he had cleared 15-5 before missing at 15-9. So he drops to 63 points behind his record pace.

He goes to lie on a rubdown table inside the training tent. "I should have made it," he says. "I had the height. So much for the record. If I'd jumped at 15-5, I might have had a chance. But I can't see it now."

4:30 P.M.

With three throws in the javelin, Jenner can suddenly see the record again. He had thrown 214-11 in August while chasing Avilov's record. Now, needing only a fair throw to ensure a spot in the top three, he throws 219-3 the first time.

His second throw is 225-1.

The next day, an Oregon newspaper will print a photograph of Jenner's face before he released his third throw. It will show his eyes focused on a point just a few inches away from the tip of the javelin. Within the limits of his power and strength, it is a perfect throw, and it travels 227 feet, 3 inches, before the tip hits the earth.

Dixon, throwing with a black rubber brace on his elbow, fouls on his first throw, makes 200-8 on his second, and then passes the third. Jenner, with 871 points, goes into first place with a total of 7,821. Dixon is 73 points behind but is assured of a place on the team. And four others—Samara, Gough, Hancock, and Brigham—are only two points apart in the race for third.

"I don't know how fast I can run it," Jenner tells me. "If I feel good, I'll try to get it. But I don't know, I really don't know."

After his superb throws in the javelin, he needs to run under 4:14 to break his own world record. But somebody has had another idea. The officials will take the 14.3 hand-timed mark in the hurdles and apply it toward a world record. That gives Jenner another 30 points, which means that he needs only 4:18 for a world record.

"Fine," he says to this. "Fine. Whatever. I'll run as fast as I can."

The seven highest scorers are put together in the last heat of the 1500. That includes the five athletes still in contention for third place. Roger George, though in seventh place, would have to make up just 80 points on Gough, Samara, Brigham, and Hancock, and he is a better distance runner than the rest.

"Follow me," Jenner tells Samara a few seconds before the gun.

Jenner goes stomping off alone and into the lead. No other decathlete in the country runs this race as well as he. George tries to keep pace, but falls behind. Samara pulls in behind George and the others drop farther away, losing ground with every step. Again, here in the evening, all the other events have ended and the decathletes are alone on the track. Sportscaster Jim McKay, taping for an ABC-TV broadcast, stands in the middle of the track near the first turn, and Jenner nearly brushes his shoulders as he goes pounding into the last lap. Jenner leads by nearly half the length of the back straight. His eyes are wide and his mouth is pulled open so that he can gulp in the air. Behind him, Samara is staring at George's back, letting his eyes wander only long enough to look up at his wife in the stands on the last lap, with an expression that is equally pained and triumphant. Then he fixes on George's back, knowing that he must stay within 12 seconds.

The noise has been building for the last two laps. It crests as Jenner crosses the line with the scoreboard timer showing 4:16. It subdues and then rises again as George and Samara cross the line, Samara obviously close enough to have clinched third place, because Hancock and Brigham are running last, still in the far turn as Samara comes across the finish line.

Jenner's time is just fast enough to qualify for a record and slow enough to create complications. He is credited with three different scores.

His meet score, recorded at 8,507, has been computed with hand timing in the 100 meters and 1500 meters, automatic timing in the 400 meters and the hurdles, with credit for the wind-aided long jump.

Another score, of 8,444, is computed with automatic timing in each race, without credit for the wind-aided jump. That leaves him 10 points behind Avilov's automatic score of 8,454.

A third score is computed with hand timing in all the races, again discounting the wind-aided long jump, for a total of 8,538 points, 14 over his own world record. And that apparently is good enough for the meet officials, for they are filling in the blanks on a yellow world-record certification form within five minutes after Jenner has crossed the line in the 1500 meters.

June 27, 1976

I was happy with what I did. Not because of the record, which didn't impress me all that much, but in being able to score so well without the nice, nervous edge I usually need to perform. For example, the high jump. When I missed my first two jumps at 6-8, I didn't feel as though I was backed up against a wall. I didn't hear that little voice inside me saying, let's go, you've got to make this one. And I didn't make it. But I will when I'm into the Games.

The last week before the Trials was pure hell. I was worried about my hamstring. That bothered me right until I left for Eugene.

After I ran the 100 within a couple of tenths of what Samara and Dixon did, I stopped worrying about what the rest of them were doing. I knew that as long as I went out and did certain performances, right down the line, then I'd make it on the team. In the Games, it'll be different. I won't be able to get away from what Avilov and Dixon do. I can't figure on making a certain mark and knowing positively that it'll be good enough to win the gold. I'll have to watch the scores, then let that motivate me to do better in certain events.

I feel good because I don't believe this was an especially good meet. My shot was terrible, but I'd better get used to it, the way the fingers feel. I didn't vault well, either. My long jump could have been better. And even with all that, I wound up doing as well as Avilov ever did on his very best day. That's got to make him think. That'll give him something to worry about when he reads the paper at breakfast tomorrow morning. I'm sure it will give him a big shot of adrenaline when he finds out. I know how I'd feel if I found out that he had just scored 8,500 points. It would psych me up tremendously. It wouldn't scare me, but it would sure make me anxious to get out and run a few extra miles while I've still got the chance.

Only one thing bothers me. It's that 1500. Once I got out there, knowing I had a chance to beat the record, I started pushing. I gave it everything I've got. I really don't think I can run any harder. And I came up with a 4:16. That's not crummy but it disappoints me. The way I've always pictured it happening at Montreal, I'd be 50, maybe 100 points down to Avilov and maybe to Dixon going into the 1500. I've always figured that I'd have to run just a super race, run a 4:10 if I had to. I've never doubted that I could.

Until now, anyway. I just don't know if I can run any faster. If I can't, I might be in big trouble.

He seemed tired but happy that night when he joined a party of about 30 friends and family at a steak house in Eugene. He wore a blue brushed-denim suit with "BRUZER" stitched in burgundy embroidery across the shoulders. His mother and Chrystie's parents and cousins had come to Eugene to watch him compete. So had his coach, Weldon, and they all sat together at a long table. It seemed less a victory celebration than an appreciation. It was the sort of affair to which a proud family without much money might treat a son after his high school graduation.

The Last Month

Jenner began jogging two days after he ran at Eugene. But his serious distance training was finished. That extracted too great a toll in energy and strength, and he wanted to be rested before Montreal. He continued to lift weights and work on his technique in all the field events except the shot put. The injured tendon in his left hand still was too painful.

In his mailbox one day was a letter from the U.S. Olympic Committee. The first paragraph congratulated him on winning a place on the U.S. team. The second ordered him to report to Plattsburgh, New York, to begin training with the U.S. track and field team no later than July 6.

June 30, 1976

I'll go, but I resent it. I don't like being ordered around like that. It's senseless to go running off to Plattsburgh when my home is here, all my training facilities are here. I'd much rather stay home until the last possible day. Maybe that way I have a chance of keeping my head on straight. Once I get up there, it'll be impossible to get away from it all. I won't be able to think of anything but the Games.

I'll go, mostly because it'll be more of a hassle to stay away. They'll be calling every day and pestering me. I'll get up there with plenty of time. At least a couple of hours to spare before midnight of the sixth.

Jenner copes so well with pressure that it seems to have no effect. He contains it within himself, and his demeanor rarely betrays him. Even during the last few days before the Trials, he had been open and accessible. Exactly four weeks before he would compete at Montreal, he spoke about his chances without hesitation or false bravado. He was almost coldly analytical, as though he were discussing an athlete and a decathlon in which he had no stake.

July 1, 1976

About the conditions, I don't know much. Neither does anybody else. I know the stadium is almost completely enclosed, except for a roof, which means negligible wind. And the chances are that the weather will be hot and humid. I don't know if the track will be as fast as the one at Eugene, though it shouldn't matter. The conditions will be the same for everybody.

I'd like to at least stay even with Avilov in the 100. I'd be looking good if I could beat him by a tenth or two-tenths. He'll get some back in the long jump for sure. And then the shot. Right now I can't count on throwing much better than 46 feet in the shot. That hurts. That means Avilov will pick up some points on me there. Usually I can count on out-throwing him by at least a foot. Before the Trials, I'd have said that I couldn't possibly win if I threw just 46 feet in the shot. Now I don't know. The way I'm running the 400 and throwing the javelin lately, maybe I could get away with it. He'll outjump me for sure in the high jump, and the only question is by how much. And then the quarter. A year ago I wouldn't have said so, but now I think I can beat him by a second, maybe more. I feel confident about the 400 now, after beating Dixon. He was ready to run up in Eugene.

Ideally, I'll be within 100 points of Avilov after the first day. If I'm that close, I'm in really good shape.

He'll beat me for sure in the hurdles. But the discus has been good to me lately. I'll start to catch him there. I don't have room for just another 15-1 in the vault. I need 15-9, and I'll have to beat him by at least a foot. We've been pretty even in the javelin until just recently. But now maybe I can count on gaining some points there. Then the 1500. The only guy who runs it faster than I can is Litvinenko. He's done a 4:05. I don't expect him to be close enough to me after nine events to make any difference. But if he is, I'm in trouble. No way will I pick up any points on Litvinenko in the 1500.

It's going to be a tremendously competitive decathlon. Look at all those guys who have scored over 8,100— Kratschmer, Grebeniuk, Zeilbauer, Katus. There have never been so many guys scoring so well before an Olympics. Never near it. The winning score in 1968 was 8,194. We've already got seven, eight guys who have scored more than that this year. Avilov set the record in 1972, but the scores dropped off drastically after that. Litvinenko won the silver with just 8,035, and third place was 7,989.

All those high scores are an indication of potential, but it can be so tough to perform up to your potential under the conditions that the Games impose. Putting it all together in the Olympics the way Avilov did in 1972, having the greatest decathlon of your life, is a long-shot thing. That's especially true of somebody who's being exposed to the Olympics for the first time. That's why when I lie in bed at night and wonder how it's going to go, I always consider Avilov the biggest threat. He's done it before. He's proven himself. Kratschmer scored that 8,380, but he had to go about 250 points over his best to do it. Same with Zeilbauer. He's never scored anywhere close to that 8,310 he had a couple of months ago. Dixon probably has more

*talent than any of us. If his vaulting keeps getting better, if
he brings it all together for two days, he could do it, no
doubt about it. I've been waiting for it to happen for two
years, showing up at a meet and waiting for Dixon to blow
me away.*

*But the truth . . . the truth is, I don't see myself losing. I
recognize the possibility, and I'm ready to deal with it if it
happens, but when I imagine what happens up in Montreal
I see myself winning. When I think of how my life is going to
be a month from now, when this is all over, I see myself
having won the gold medal. I've traveled all over the
world. I've beaten every single one of the guys who have
any chance of winning. I've proven that I can score more
points than any one of them, and I've done all that I
possibly can to make that happen. I should win. There's no
doubt in my mind. There is no physical reason why I
shouldn't win the gold medal.*

That same day, the Canadian government announced that it
would bar Taiwanese athletes if the team carried a Chinese
flag in the opening ceremonies or claimed to represent
China. The International Olympic Committee then threat-
ened to remove its sanction from the Games. On July 2 the
U.S. Olympic Committee announced that it would not send a
team if the IOC removed its Olympic sanction. At about the
time that this announcement was made known to the press,
Bruce Jenner was clearing 16 feet, one inch, while practicing
his pole vault.

July 3, 1976

*That stuff doesn't bother me. I don't pay any attention to it.
It crops up all the time, and nothing ever comes of it. There
shouldn't be any place for that crap. That's not what it's all
about.*

No, I wouldn't have let it stop me. If the United States

138

hadn't sent a team, I'd have shown up on my own. I've worked too hard to let somebody take my chance away like that. I'll run, no matter what. That'll be my own way of protesting.

(James Gilkes, a runner from Guiana, later asked to run as an individual after his nation withdrew from the Games as part of a boycott by African nations in a dispute separate from the Taiwan controversy. Gilkes offered to march in the opening parade either without a banner or under the Olympic flag. His request was denied by the International Olympic Committee.)

The day before he was to leave for Plattsburgh, Jenner washed and waxed his Porsche, parked it inside a carport next to the apartment, and then covered it with a heavy fitted cloth wrapper. That night he packed his suitcase, taking with him several changes of casual clothes, a toilet kit, seven different pairs of Adidas competition shoes, and three weeks' daily rations of vitamins already sorted into individual plastic bags.

He and Chrystie already had decided that the dog, Bertha, would fly with them. Chrystie a month earlier had arranged for all the necessary papers for a dog to enter Canada from the United States. So along with their luggage they checked a large portable cage containing one large golden Labrador retriever.

I'd thought about it for years and years, getting ready to leave home and go off to compete for the gold medal. I was very conscious of what I was about to do, and how important it would be to me for the rest of my life, knowing that when I next returned home, the outcome would be settled and I would never be able to change it.

I thought about it when I parked the car and covered it up. I thought, the next time I sit in this car, I want to be the Olympic champion. We were just about to leave when one of our friends came by and dropped off a bottle of cham-

139

pagne. He said that when we got home from Montreal, he wanted Bertha, Chrystie, and me to take a bath in this to celebrate. We put it in the refrigerator to chill. I thought about that bottle often when I was at Montreal, even during the competition. I knew what would happen if I lost and came home to it. I wouldn't even want to open the refrigerator, because it would be there, mocking me, every time I did.

Finally, when we left the house, I remember closing the door behind me, thinking to myself, "It'll all be over the next time you open up the door." We were flying to Montreal, with a connection in Chicago. Then we were going to take a bus from Montreal down to Plattsburgh. On the flight from Chicago, there were about a dozen athletes from different parts of the country who all knew each other. We were laughing and having a good time but I couldn't really get into it. I kept looking out of the window, getting emotional, thinking about how much I wanted to win.

I got myself into trouble that way as soon as we landed at Montreal. We were in line, going through customs and immigration. Everybody else, all the athletes, got a little tag and went right through. But somebody marked a big "X" on mine and I got pulled off to the side. One of the inspectors asked me who I was and how long I expected to be in Montreal. Naturally I said, "I'm on the American team and I'll be here until the end of the Games." That was wrong, of course. I was supposed to get on a bus and go to Plattsburgh, but I never thought to tell him that. I was thinking, "Wow, here I am, finally in Montreal; here's where it's going to happen." They took me off to a little room and sat me down. You've got to remember that se- curity was awfully tight for the Games. Somebody in the room wanted to see my credentials with the U.S. team. I didn't have any. That's one of the things I was supposed to get in Plattsburgh. They put me through the mill for a while before they finally let me go.

It was a hot, muggy, miserable night in Plattsburgh. I was wishing I had stayed home a while longer. I went straight to my room at the dormitory in the state university, where the team was staying. My family has friends in Plattsburgh, and Chrystie and Bertha went off to stay with them.

All I wanted was peace, but instead what we got was a lot of red tape and standing in lines. The next morning was another terrifically hot day. I met the two Freds, Samara and Dixon, and ran some in the morning. And then we had to go through processing. Later we had our fittings for the Olympic clothing, the parade uniforms and the competition suits. The athletes were supposed to arrive at one o'clock in the afternoon. Samara, Dixon and I were right on time. We stood in line to pick up our socks, shoes, jocks, shorts, sweats, and our suitcases. That all went fast enough. Next we were supposed to wait to be fitted by a tailor for the regulation leisure suit for the parade. We stood three hours in line at that point and didn't move 15 feet. Later we found out that there weren't enough tailors. Beautiful. We're supposed to be training for the Olympics and instead we're standing in line three hours. I hate to sound like a prima donna, complaining. But when a big meet gets this close, it blocks out everything else in my mind. There's no room for anything else. I get angry at the little inconveniences and intrusions that I normally take as a matter of course. Then it was time for a physical. We had our I.D. pictures taken, got our teeth checked.

I had mixed feelings about the training conditions at the college. The main outdoor track was just horrible, some kind of rubberized asphalt surface that came up in little bits as we ran on it with our spikes. I could run and feel myself digging up the track. I was sorry for the runners,

*like the quarter-milers. But there was a neat 130-yard
Tartan track inside the gymnasium and all the jumping
and vaulting facilities were perfect. So I stayed away from
the outdoor track, sprinted a little on the grass, pole-
vaulted once or twice, and threw the discus.*

*Then one day about a week before the opening cere-
monies, the track team boarded buses and went up to
Montreal for a workout at a practice track there. I got
pretty psyched as the bus got close to the city; I looked
across the St. Lawrence River at the skyline, then picked
out the Olympic Village and the stadium.*

*I was wondering whether I had recovered from the
Trials. It had been only two weeks since the competition in
Eugene, and it takes a while to recuperate. I threw the
discus and generally felt pretty dead. I worked on the
hurdles. Then Dixon and Samara and I did a running
workout together, and that was different. We decided we
would run a 330, a 220, and a 165. These are distances that
we all run in practice. But it was a more competitive
situation with them running beside me. We ran the 330 and
we all finished pretty much together. My time was 34 flat, a
p.r. We ran a 220 with a walking start, just walking up to
the line and then taking off. And I ran. I did a 21.5.
Another p.r. Fantastic. So we ran the 165. The best I'd
ever done until that day was 15.7. This time I ran 15.3.
Never, ever, have I had a running workout like this one. I
was thinking to myself, "I did that? Me?"*

Several days still remained before they were to leave
Plattsburgh. Jenner ran easy, relatively short distances in the
mornings and practiced his vaulting, jumping, and discus.
One day he tried the shot put; the tendon still hurt. Chrystie
came to visit every day with the dog. He listened to rumors of
overcrowding in the Village, stories that were supposed to
have trickled down from the early arrivals, the swimmers and
the gymnasts.

I heard the stories. It was supposed to be like a tenement, a half dozen people in each room. Some guys were saying that they were going to move out, find another place to stay, just as soon as they got there and checked in.

So I talked to a coach and he promised to let me find another place if it really was as bad as everybody was saying. But he told me to hold off until we actually got up there and took a good look. I didn't care about where I stayed, as long as it didn't get in the way of what I was up there to do. I just wanted peace, no hassles, but I was afraid that if the Village was as bad as some people said, that it would interfere.

We were supposed to be assigned to rooms alphabetically, but we were told that we could switch our assignments if we could agree on it. The Village was built like an apartment complex so that it could be rented or sold as condominiums later. There were 12 athletes to each two-bedroom, one-bath apartment, but it turned out to be not so bad as it sounds. A group of us track and field athletes got together and decided to share one apartment. We were all friends and acquaintances. I knew the others were all serious athletes, that they wouldn't be loud or rowdy. So while we were still in Plattsburgh, we made a deal to grab an apartment together when we got to the Village.

The group included pole-vaulters Dave Roberts and Earl Bell, discus specialist John Powell, and shot-putter Pete Schmock, javelin-throwers Sam Colson and Richard George, hammer-thrower Larry Hart, steeplechase runner Henry Marsh, and high-jumper James Barrineau, plus the three decathletes.

There was no big rivalry among me and the other two decathletes. Samara was a bit more competitive than Dixon or I. He would be more verbal if he had a good workout, while Dixon might run a super-fast 400 and say very little

143

about it. They're my friends. I like them both and respect
them.

But just the same, there were times when I wasn't too
keen on sharing an apartment with them. I go through a lot
of little things just before a meet that I didn't especially
want them to see. No big secrets, nothing that's going to
help them score more points, just little things that I'd
rather keep private. Like putting a chair out in the middle
of the room and pretending it's a hurdle, walking through
the motions the way I do at home with my real hurdle.
When the two Freds were around, I felt funny doing that.

Three days before the team was to leave Plattsburgh for the
Village, President Ford visited the camp. Jenner strutted
rather proudly through the cordon of police and Secret Service around the track. The athletes were separated into small
clumps around the perimeter of the field. Some were asked to
perform as the President strolled from one group to another.
Jenner seemed relieved at not being asked to high-jump or
pole-vault when the President walked over to the decathletes
and posed for a photograph with them. The President shook
hands and mentioned that he knew something about the
decathlon, for Bob Mathias had been elected for three terms
to the Republican side of the House of Representatives at the
same time Ford was representing his district in Michigan.

Jenner remembers the visit as a pleasant interlude. He also
remembers that it cost him a half-day's training time.

The next day the track and field team was off to Montreal,
again for a one-day visit. This time they would compete in a
practice meet on a training field beside the Olympic stadium.

It was cold and rainy, and I went up just to run the
hurdles. I was pretty skeptical about the whole idea. I was
still thinking about my hamstring. All I needed was to run
with my legs still tight, here in this cold weather, then slip
or maybe whack out a leg muscle. But there was one neat

moment. As I stood in the blocks and then looked down the lanes, at the hurdles lined up nice and straight, I was also looking beyond, right at the Olympic Stadium. I couldn't avoid it. I ran straight at it. I liked that. It made me realize again how close it was all getting to be. I liked just being there near it, knowing that it was real and that I'd be running there soon.

I didn't run a good race. I was doing okay for about the first six hurdles, running right with Dixon. But I hit the seventh hurdle with my trailing leg, really banged it, and that slowed me up. I decided to take it easy and finished with a 15.1. But I felt better when I found out Dixon had done a 14.4. My last two hurdles are usually my best and I figured that I'd have run about the same as Dixon if I hadn't slowed up. So that made me feel better. I had the speed and the technique. All I needed was to get a little excited.

Dixon was busy. He ran 14.4 in the hurdles, threw the shot 50 feet, and ran 48.7 in the quarter. I was impressed. At that point, I figured he would be in contention. The only thing that made me doubt it was the way he kept telling me that all the pressure was off now that he had made the team. He said something like, "Everything I do from now on is a bonus." That was like my attitude at Munich. I was grateful just to be there. But that isn't the way to score a lot of points, either. A couple of times I felt like telling him, "Fred, it's just beginning." But on the other hand, I felt very selfishly, "Great, you keep thinking that way and I know who's going to be in better shape when we get to a tough spot." That's the difference that comes from having been to the Olympics once before.

They took a bus back to Plattsburgh that evening, rested the next day, and then prepared to leave for the Village on the Wednesday before opening ceremonies. It was a long day. It began early in the morning as the athletes' luggage was searched by security crews and then loaded onto buses. There was the trip to Montreal—about 90 miles from Plattsburgh—this time with armed escort. Jenner recalls looking from the window of the bus to see several helicopters hovering over the Canadian Customs and Immigration building at the border. The copters and a squad of motorcycle cops (whipping back and forth through traffic, running ahead to stand guard at bridges and overpasses, and then buzzing back to pick up the convoy) led the entourage into the city. Then a long wait at the security gate of the Village, waiting for still another search of the luggage. Wandering to find the appointed apartment, then appropriating a bedroom with a view of the stadium. Wandering with Dixon down empty staircases, through obscure passageways, into a basement before finally stumbling into the dining room for dinner.

And still the most important part of the day was to come. There was to be another practice meet at the nearby training field. Jenner would throw the discus, pole-vault, and run one leg of a 1600-meter relay team. This was an open competition, not strictly for decathletes, so he would be running, jumping, and throwing against specialists from around the world. Jenner felt surprisingly strong. His three throws in the discus measured 164, 170, and 163 feet, though he barely fouled on the second throw by letting a foot slip out of the throwing circle. There was no wind.

He vaulted 15 feet on his first attempt, cleared 15-5 on his first try, then made 15-9 and took three tries at 16-1, missing each time. He recalls a proud flush at realizing that artist Leroy Neiman was sketching him on a drawing pad as he vaulted. Then he went off to run the relay race.

The three decathletes and Mark Lutz, the 200-meter specialist, were supposed to run as a team in the 1600-meter relay race, each of us running 400 meters. But Lutz pulled out because he was having trouble with his leg and he was afraid it would bother him. Then Dixon pulled out and Samara pulled out and that left just me. And I wanted to run 400 meters. So I got the coaches to stick me on a team. They had me running third leg on a team with Fred Newhouse leading off and Maxie Parks second. I thought, oh, no! I knew we'd be leading the race when I got the baton. You can't find two guys in the whole world who will run two legs of a 1600-meter relay faster than those two. So I'm running the third lap and I'm going to be passing off to Edwin Moses, who eventually won the gold medal in the 400-meter hurdles. There was another team from the United States, with another good quarter-miler, James Robinson, running the third leg same as me. Then there was a team from Trinidad and another from Kenya, since this was before the African boycott.

Sure enough, Newhouse and Parks really got moving, and we had the lead by about three yards when I took the baton. Through the turn, down the backstretch, I was holding the lead. I felt great. I didn't get passed until the last turn, and they still didn't run away from me. I asked somebody what the time had been on my leg. He said 47.4. I'd never broken 48 before, so that was a lot faster than I'd ever run the 400 meters. You get a running start in a relay race, but that's worth just a couple of tenths, if anything. Not that much. It was still the fastest by far that I'd ever run the distance. I walked over to Chrystie and asked her what she had gotten on her stopwatch. This is her job, and she takes it pretty seriously. But she didn't want to tell me. Her watch said 47.5 and she was sure that she had made a mistake, because it was incredibly fast.

I felt good that night. The 400 is so important. Run that well, and you know that you've got the speed for the sprints and the endurance to run the 1500, because the 400 takes both speed and stamina. I knew then that if anybody was going to beat me, they'd have to score a lot of points.

From that day on, everything is kind of blank, except for the opening ceremonies. Mostly I sat around, thought

*about my technique, got my head straight. My body was as
good as it was going to be and now I just needed to get my
mind in shape.*

The Canadian National Film Board, for its documentary on
the Games, had decided to choose six athletes from different
sports and different nations and follow them through the
ceremonies and through the competition. Jenner was one of
the six. So his attire for the opening ceremonies included not
only his standard issue socks, shoes, and Montgomery Ward
double-knit leisure suit, but also a remote microphone. He
was dogged throughout the day by several cameramen. But,
he remembers gratefully, they didn't ask him to do anything.
He would have preferred to skip the opening ceremonies
altogether. (Neither Avilov nor Kratschmer marched in the
parade; rumor was that their respective nations had seques-
tered them outside Montreal.) At Munich, he had stood on
his feet more than five hours during the ceremonies. But
because of the African boycott and the Canadians' obdurate
stand on the Taiwanese, the parade was shorter this time. He
waited only three hours in the staging area and on the
stadium floor. He was surprised to find that the music and the
pomp did not move him as they had in Munich. But he had
done this all before and he approached this as a very important business trip. He searched for Chrystie in the stands
and, amazingly, found her. She was jumping in her seat and
waving her arms. He waved back to her. She had picked him
out easily, for he was the only American athlete being followed by a personal crew of film cameramen. Then he returned to his room, but his legs had lost too much on the
stadium floor for him to attempt a workout.

*Avilov and Kratschmer didn't show up until four or five
days before the competition. I thought about them often,
wondering how their workouts were going, but I never
heard. I did hear some stories about Kratschmer. Some of*

the U.S. athletes had gone to train with the West Germans at their camp up near Quebec City. They came back telling me about all the doctors the Germans had up there, how far advanced their sports medicine was, how much they were doing for all the athletes. I thought, oh, nuts, they're pumping this Kratschmer up into some kind of a monster. I hadn't thought too much about him until then. I'd seen him compete once before, in the meet at Tallinn. I thought he had a lot of undeveloped talent, but I was surprised to hear that he had scored so many points in Austria. I never did see him until the morning of the first day of competition.

And though I never heard what Avilov was running or saw him work out seriously, I did run into him about five days before we were going to run. It was at the practice track. I'd gone to do some running, and I saw Litvinenko and Grebeniuk standing off to the side of the track. Litvinenko called out my name, and I waved hello to him while I looked for Avilov. I knew he couldn't be too far away. Then I spotted him jogging around the track.

The press and all the insiders had been building the decathlon up as a personal confrontation between Avilov and me. It wasn't just the Olympic championship, it was Jenner against Avilov. I was very aware of that, as I'm sure he was. It made for a difficult situation between the two of us when we met face to face. But I think we handled it well.

He was wearing a big droopy moustache that I hadn't seen before, so I put a hand up to my upper lip. He started to laugh. He ran over and we started to talk, just kidding each other. I don't speak any Russian, and I don't know how much English he understands, but he manages to get his point across when he wants to.

"Avilov," I told him, "you look good, real strong."

"And you look big and strong, also, Jenner," he said.

"Oh, no," I said. "My hurdles are very weak. Terrible. My style is very bad."

"And me, my long jump is so bad," he said.

Then we looked at each other out of the corner of our eyes and we started laughing. We just cracked up. There was no way either one of us was going to psych out the other, not at that point.

I like Avilov. We're not buddies, by any means. But you get a feeling for the people you're competing against and I have the feeling that Avilov is a good man. If the circumstances were different, we might have been friends.

Still, I never did see Avilov train hard. I was curious to hear some of his workout times, but it didn't bother me not to know. I was feeling pretty confident after that practice meet. I knew I'd be scoring an awful lot of points.

His concern about Avilov may have been greater than he cares to admit. Chrystie kept a sporadic journal beginning one week before the competition. This is an excerpt from an entry dated July 23:

"Countdown," she writes. "Seven more days. When I think about it my stomach goes into a flip flop. Bruce's waves of moodiness are more frequent and harder to predict. Something little can send him into a scowled countenance . . . [or] into cheerfulness. I learn more every day about how to be a cheerful and calming influence.

"[Bruce and I] went to dinner with Vince and Ernie. Good friends—lots of laughing and fun. Great Italian food; Bruce's favorite and important 'carbos.' . . . We made the *stupid* mistake of talking about Avilov, and Bruce quit eating. I wish he would speak up about what we are doing. I had to be alert and say to him, 'We shouldn't be talking about this—you're not eating' and he immediately and angrily agreed. 'Enough other people talk about it; why must you?' he said. 'Who cares where Avilov is?'

"*Very defensive.* We changed the subject."

It was one of his few excursions out of the apartment. Only once between the opening ceremonies and the decathlon did he visit the stadium, and that was to watch his friends Powell and Wilkins in the discus finals.

Occasionally he left the Village to visit Chrystie and the dog in their motel room, just across the street. (She had gone to retrieve Bertha in Plattsburgh because Bruce had mentioned several times that he wanted to have the dog with him. At this point, a whim was tantamount to a command. "He is very secure when he cuddles with her," Chrystie noted in her journal. A portrait of a boy and his dog.) Mostly, though, he stayed in the room, leaving only to eat in the dining hall. Each apartment at the Village had a TV monitor on which the athletes could select either the ABC network feed, Canadian Broadcasting Company coverage, or various remote transmissions. Bruce watched every day. He was watching even more intently than usual on a rainy Monday afternoon three days before the beginning of the decathlon. Two of his friends and roommates, Earl Bell and Dave Roberts, were jumping in the pole vault finals. Bell held the world record until Roberts took it away a month earlier at the Trials in Eugene. They were expected to finish 1-2 at the Games. But in a rain that fluctuated between drizzle and downpour, Bell was completely shut out of the medals and Roberts finished with a bronze.

That upset me. I was so angry and disturbed that I turned off the set and walked out onto the balcony, trying to deal with what I had just seen. It was a wet and ugly day, and I was disgusted. For once, I was not worried about catching a cold or anything like that. I just stood out there in the rain. It looked like everybody in our apartment was going down the tubes. You look at the talent in that single apartment and it's not too much to expect two or three gold medals and a couple of silvers. But as the days went by, the place got more and more gloomy. Pete Schmock was out of the medals. Powell finished with a bronze. Here were

Roberts and Bell, now, ending up with just a bronze between them.

Watching something like that, it has to shake you up. It scared me to watch a guy like Roberts make one mistake and end up in third place. This guy is the best pole-vaulter in the world. Nobody would seriously dispute that. Yet because of the rain, here he is, coming back with a bronze medal. It made me think: the same thing could happen to you, Jenner. I know I'm the best in the world at what I do. I've been the best in the world for two years, but that didn't mean a thing. That was pressure right there.

And I was bugged at seeing what was happening to the U.S. track and field team. I'm no super-patriot but I sure got tired of hearing the East German anthem and the Russian anthem being played over and over again. I run for myself, and I meant it when I said that if the United States pulled out of the Games, I'd have tried to compete as an individual. But at the same time, I can't deny the fact that I'm an American and that I think I live in the best country in the world. I've had a chance to do what I'm best at, to go as far as my own abilities would take me. I don't know that I'd have been able to do that elsewhere. And I'm also very aware that no matter what my own motivations are, there are millions of people out there who put their hopes in me, identify with me, just because I'm wearing a uniform that says "USA" across the front.

I remember the first time I got a USA warm-up suit and uniform, just before Munich in 1972. Oh, man, I was proud. I remember that I went back to my room, tried them on to see how they fit, and stood in front of a mirror to see how I looked in them. So now, knowing and remembering all that, I couldn't help but feel that I was part of a team, be aware of what was happening to the team, and feel some kind of responsibility to the country and the people.

Now all this was running through my head as I stood out there in the rain. Pete Schmock came out with me. He said

*a funny thing that probably sounds pretty trite, but I
swear it happened.*

*He said: "Bruce, it looks like you're going to have to
carry us now."*

*It didn't sound trite or corny to me at the time, as
emotional as I was. I'd been thinking the same thing, and I
knew that he wasn't talking just about the athletes in our
one apartment. I just nodded at him, said, "Yeah, you're
right." There wasn't a heck of a lot to say to it. I looked out
at the stadium, so grey and murky in the drizzle. I was
thinking that my turn there would come in so few days.
Then I really began to feel the pressure. Now it wasn't just
the pressure to do well for myself, to make something out of
all the time and effort Chrystie and I had put into it. On top
of it all, I felt I had to carry the country, too. That's when I
started to get my psyche up. I don't think I ever lost it.*

Chrystie recalls:

"Bruce showed up at the motel room that evening. I felt so
bad for Dave Roberts. I had kind of a personal stake in it,
since I'd been staying with Roberts' girlfriend. My own room
was miles from the Village, but she let me stay there with her,
so close to the stadium and the Village. I was surprised to see
Bruce there since he'd been spending so much time in his
room. I sensed that he wanted to talk, so we went out to eat.
When we sat down and everything was quiet he blurted it
out, that he was shaken up by what happened to Roberts and
that he felt he had the whole weight of the team and the
country on his shoulders. He was very serious about it. And
all of a sudden, I felt so sorry for the poor guy. Whether it was
true or not, that's how he felt. He sounded so forlorn and
alone when he said it. Really sad. I wanted to reach out and
touch him. But what could I do? What could anybody do?"

I don't doubt that his feeling was sincere. He is not a
cynical man, and given the circumstances of the moment,
that sense of responsibility seems natural and credible.

Surely, Roberts' experience must have been sobering for one in Jenner's position. But Jenner admits that he runs best under pressure. Secretly, he may have welcomed the self-imposed burden. And perhaps it is not too farfetched to suggest that this was a device to accomplish what he had been trying to do for a week: to hone his mind to the same edge that his body had already reached. His own words: *"That's when I started to get my psyche up. I don't think I ever lost it."*

And even with his sense of patriotic responsibility, he was never far from his personal ambition and desire.

I knew this was my last meet and I wanted to finish right. I didn't want to go out a loser. If you go out and win, I told myself, the rest of your life may be very exciting. Lose, finish number two, and you're going to have a very dull life.

The first time I saw Roberts after he had lost, I didn't know what to say. Nobody ever does, to somebody who's just lost something that was important to them. I could just see that, coming home with a silver medal. I wouldn't hear the phone or the doorbell for weeks. Not because people would think less of me as a loser. They just wouldn't know what to say. A very dull life.

On Wednesday, July 28, the day before the competition, Bruce borrowed his father-in-law's car and drove with Chrystie and Bertha out of Montreal and north to the Laurentian Mountains. Montreal was hot and full of Olympic banners and people talking about running and jumping. The mountains were cool and green and seemed far removed from the athletic madness.

They ate lunch at a lodge that overlooked a calm and lovely lake. Bruce found a wooden stick, walked out onto a pier, and tossed the stick into the water for Bertha to retrieve. But while he waited for the dog to swim back with the stick in her mouth, he went through the motions of flinging the discus.

He and Chrystie did not once mention the decathlon that afternoon. They talked about the weather and the gorgeous setting for the lake and how much Bertha loved splashing in the water.

He went to the motel room with Chrystie. They were alone there except for the dog and the telephone, which rang several times. Then Bruce left to have dinner at the Village. Before he walked out the door, he mentioned the competition for the first time.

He had been thinking about it, he said. He had decided that he would be in good shape if he could stay within 200 points of Avilov or whoever else was in first place at the end of the first day.

Then he kissed her good-bye and walked away.

The Last Mile

He had brought an alarm clock from San Jose and had set it to ring at a quarter to seven in the morning. After taking himself this far, he wasn't going to rely on someone else to wake him for the biggest day of his life. But he knew that it was an unnecessary precaution. Though he slept surprisingly well that night, he was awake well before six. He lay awake in bed for a while, stared out at the Olympic stadium in the early morning light, then pulled on a polyester sweatsuit and a pair of sandals and walked down to the dining hall.

The food had been plentiful and at least palatable since he arrived. There were no limits to the servings. Some of the shot-putters and weight lifters might pile on three or four steaks and a quart of mashed potatoes each trip through the serving line. There was also a table of fruit, and many of the Eastern Europeans would stuff their pockets with oranges and bananas, strawberries and raspberries, when they left the hall and returned to their rooms. Jenner for the last few days had stuck mainly to carbohydrates. He believed that they were more quickly assimilated than proteins. He had been doing this for years. For breakfast the morning of a meet, he preferred French toast. Chrystie tells of spending a day in the Paris markets trying to find nutmeg and cinnamon so that she could prepare that dish for his breakfast before the 1975 French Championships. The French chef at the dormitory had never heard of this "French toast." But he gave Chrystie the run of the kitchen, and the young French athletes gathered curiously around as Chrystie cooked and Bruce ate this concoction. If this was what the American champion had for breakfast, perhaps it was not all bad . . .

This morning there is no French toast in the big recessed aluminum trays at the steam table. He takes pancakes and orange juice, sits alone at a table, but eats little. His stomach is queasy, and that does not surprise him.

He returns to the apartment about the same time that Samara and Dixon are dressing for breakfast. He goes to his room, spends more time than he needs gathering up his equipment, stuffing it all into a canvas bag. He takes towels, a glass jug of Gatorade from which he has soaked off the label, two pairs of socks and five pairs of shoes, all different and all with three diagonal stripes on the sides, the trademark of the German clothing and footwear company known as Adidas. One pair is a flat-soled warm-up shoe that he wears between events. The next is a lightweight spiked sprinting shoe which he will use in the 100 meters, the 400-meter run, and also the 110-meter high hurdles the next day. There is a special pair of shoes for long-jumping, with soles slightly raised near the heels to help impart a forward rocking movement at the moment of takeoff. There is another pair with a pliable rubber bottom specially built to give him a good feel of the shot-putting and discus circle, and still another pair of which the sole in the right shoe is built higher than the left for body leverage in high-jumping. Today he leaves behind his pole-vaulting shoes (built heavier than most track shoes to prevent ripping from the strain of planting and takeoff), his high-laced javelin boots (for lateral ankle support), and a battered pair that seems to belong more at the bottom of a high school gym locker than in the equipment bag of a world-record holder. These he has owned for three years. He wears them to run the 1500 meters. He also stuffs an elastic bandage and a broader elastic body wrapping into one corner of the bag, and he is ready to leave.

He walks down to the ground floor, walks without hurry down a wide concrete walk, past a blue-shirted security officer who stands within a glass guardhouse inside the high, chain-link fence that is topped with barbed wire. Jenner goes through the gate, into a short passageway beneath the street, Rue Viau, then down a steep grassy hill cut by a wide swath of walkway. As he rounds a gentle bend in the walkway, he can see the stadium, now less than a quarter-mile distant. The first heat of the 100 meters is at 10 A.M., nearly two hours away.

I started in with my psyche first thing when I saw the stadium. I thought: this is it, this one is yours, nobody's going to take it away from you. I went for a rubdown in the training room there by the practice track. Then I started to warm up, still in two pairs of sweats. I ran a 165 on the practice track—that's half one turn and a full straight-away. Next I was going to run a 110, half a turn and just half a straight, but I was about 30 yards into it when I realized that I felt so smooth and so strong, it was pointless. It reinforced in me what I'd been feeling for a couple of weeks now. I knew enough about my body and the decathlon to know that I was going to have a good one. All the signs had been right this time. I'd even thrown the shot 48 feet in my last workout, and the hand felt fine for the first time since the spring.

There is a long and somewhat complicated passage from the practice field to the stadium. Jenner is walking alone down the tunnel when Philippe Bobin, a young French decathlete, trots to catch up with him and begins a conversation. The two had met a year earlier, during the French Championships. Now Jenner, typically, is too nice to send Bobin on his way.

Perhaps he remembers four years earlier at Munich when he was a scared 22-year-old in his first Olympics.

Now less than a half hour to go. There are things to do. There is an inspection by a technical crew from the International Olympic Committee. They examine his shoes, check the length of his spikes and the height of the soles on his high-jump shoe. They check his number on a master sheet—he has been assigned 935. The number is printed on four pieces of cloth which are sewn onto the front and back of his uniform shirt and to the sides of his uniform shorts. They also strip a small piece of adhesive tape over the brand name on the heels of his shoes.

He is in his red uniform sweatsuit, automatically performing stretch exercises and watching the first heat of the 100 meters on closed circuit television. He is inside a room with bare concrete walls beneath the stands. Avilov is in this heat, running in the fourth lane, his placing determined by draw yesterday. There is a sharp report of the starter's pistol, then another, a fraction of a second later. Someone has jumped the gun and they must try again.

Beating the pistol is impossible. The gun is wired to a sensing device. So are the starting blocks beneath the feet of each runner, with switches held open by pressure from the runner. Any movement before the trigger is pulled will register automatically with the starter.

There is a second false start; this time it may be Avilov himself who jumps early. Then a third false start. The fourth time is good, but Avilov seems anchored to the blocks. Within the first 10 yards he is a step behind the rest of the field, and he loses more ground after that. He finishes ahead of only one man, Czechoslovakian Ludek Pernica, a poor sprinter. The winner is a West German, Klaus Marek. The unofficial timer on the stadium scoreboard registers him at 10.81. In a few minutes, the results of the first heat come sliding across the electronic boards that hang high at opposite ends of the stadium. Avilov's line reads:

Avilov, Nikolay   URS   11:23   749

It must be an unsettling moment for him. His time at Munich had been 11.00, for 804 points.

There is a single false start in the second heat before Raimo Pihl, a Swede who won the U.S. collegiate championship in 1974 while studying at Brigham Young University, leads the field with a time of 10.93 seconds, for 822 points. He seems to finish in a virtual dead heat with Dixon, but the electronic timer distinguishes two-hundredths of a second between them. The difference is worth 3 points, so Dixon has 819.

Jenner has been jogging in place behind the starting line. Now the red sweatsuit comes off. He stretches, sprints fluidly halfway down the track, then walks back to the starting line to wait for the starting command.

I saw the first false start in Avilov's heat and then they called us out onto the track. I was standing behind the starting blocks for the next two false starts and I knew he was in trouble. You get so keyed up for the 100, but a couple of bad starts can destroy that concentration. It can upset you if you let it, and maybe that's what happened to Avilov. I saw that he got a bad start once they did get the race going. I wasn't in a position to judge exactly where he had finished, but I knew that he wasn't running well and that he had finished somewhere back in the pack. Marek's time wasn't especially fast and I knew that Avilov had been at least a couple of steps behind him.

Then I saw Pihl and Dixon with another slow time, over 10.9, and these guys are good sprinters. I told myself that I'd better get rolling if I wanted just a decent score.

The starter really does yell, "On your marks" and "Get set" (using the language to which he himself is most accustomed—English in this case). On the first command, the runners place their feet into the blocks and settle into a crouch with both knees still touching the ground. On the second, they rise off the ground, tensing their bodies, weight balanced between the tips of their toes and their fingers spread out before them.

The third command is the report of the pistol, firing a .22 caliber cartridge with a wad of paper jammed where a slug of lead usually is found. There is more than one blank cartridge in the gun. In Jenner's heat, the first loud snap is followed by a second. Somebody in the line has jumped early. The second shot follows the first almost immediately, but Jenner runs 40 yards down the track before he brings himself up short, brings his right hand to his mouth as though to contain a curse—or maybe it is only to wipe some sweat from the top of his lip—and turns and trots back to his starting position.

They try again, and this time there is no second shot. But Jenner might have hoped for one. He runs the first 5 yards as though churning in deep sand. He is running in lane seven, with the eighth empty—the Frenchman, Leroy, has withdrawn, having been injured while long-jumping two weeks earlier. In lane six, immediately to Jenner's left, is West German Eberhard Stroot, who quickly pulls away by the length of two strides. Jenner surges, Stroot does not increase his lead, and they finish that way, 1-2, with Stroot crossing the tape in 10.75 seconds. Jenner's time is 10.94, exactly identical to Dixon's in the second heat, for 819 points.

Jenner pulls on his sweatsuit and walks across the field with Dixon to a bench beside the twin long jump approach ramps. They wait long enough to see Samara finish second in the fourth and final heat of the sprints. Samara runs the distance in 10.85 seconds. But he still finishes at least one long stride behind the powerful, composed strides of a muscular, blond man in a West German uniform who runs the fastest time of all four heats: 10.66 seconds, for 890 points. That puts him into first place.

The computerized readout on the scoreboard identifies the West German as "Kratscamer." Jenner, though, is not deceived by the misplaced vowel. This is Guido Kratschmer, and he looks serious.

I was glad to have Stroot there beside me. He's done a 10.5 before, runs the 100 better than I do, and I figured he would be a good gauge of how well I was running it.

I tried not to let the false start get to me. I can't say that I was especially tense, and there was no more time to psych myself up. I left that behind me when I stripped off my sweats and concentrated on getting down to the end of the straightaway.

I thought I got out of the blocks really well, but Stroot pulled away at first. Then I stayed pretty close to him, I thought. My acceleration was good, but in the last 30 meters I had a tendency to straighten up. My style was falling apart but nobody was falling away from me, either. I looked up to the scoreboard for Stroot's time. It read 10.7 and I figured I wasn't more than a couple of tenths behind him. I was happy with that.

With Avilov's poor race, that meant I was three-tenths of a second faster, and that put me up on him 70 or 75 points right away. I thought to myself, I have him, there's no way the guy is beating me when he gets that far behind so early.

And just when I'm thinking that way, along comes Kratschmer. I started worrying when I saw his time in that fourth heat, because he's very, very strong in the next event, the long jump. I could just see him blasting one way out there and giving me all kinds of catching up to do. So I was right back where I started, spending the first day trying not to fall too far behind.

The two runways, parallel and separated by a narrow strip of ground, end at the same pit of loose sand where the athletes land after their jump. The dual runways are supposed to save time; one decathlete can make a practice run while another prepares to jump. By draw, Dixon, Avilov, Kratschmer, and Jenner all jump on the same runway.

Dixon jumps 6.72 meters—a half-inch over 22 feet—his first time down. Avilov, Kratschmer, and Jenner jump in succession, with Avilov going 7.52 meters (24-8), Kratschmer falling 5 inches short of that at 7.39, and Jenner more than 19 inches behind Avilov at 7.05.

Avilov's jump in the second round is even longer. But the toe of his right foot touches on the wrong side of the foul board across the lane. A yellow-jacketed official standing beside the line shoots up his right arm with a small red flag held in the fist. Foul. Kratschmer also fouls the second time. Jenner improves his mark by 2 centimeters, less than an inch. But on the third try, after both Avilov and Kratschmer have failed to improve, Jenner gathers speed on his approach, jumps higher, and stays in the air longer than he ever has. One arm stabs at the air so that he is leaning forward as he hits, and the momentum of the jump carries him headfirst with only a stumble, out of the pit. The tape is stretched out. A small revolving scoreboard on the field, near the jump pit, is changed to read: 935-7.22. That is 23 feet, 8¼ inches. Jenner has jumped farther only once, when using a somersault technique that was banned as too dangerous in 1973.

Avilov's first jump is the longest of the day. But neither he nor Kratschmer come close to the 25-foot jumps of which they are capable, and which Jenner had expected of them. Dixon, meanwhile, never reaches 7 meters. His best jump of 22 feet, 8 inches, is more than 2 feet short of his p.r. For one who relies on a strong first day, it is a fatal failure.

Jenner had hoped to cut his losses. He has succeeded.

The standings after two events:

1. Kratschmer   1.789
2. Stroot   1,764
3. Marek   1,719
6. Jenner   1,684
8. Avilov   1,674
13. Dixon   1,621

Until the last week before the Games, Jenner had feared that he would lose points to Avilov and Dixon in the shot put. But then the throwing hand healed quickly, almost miraculously. He had missed three months' training but he felt ready to throw the shot near 50 feet again. His first throw is 14.96 meters, just over 49 feet. The second is short of that, but the third measures 15.35, a new p.r. by 4 inches. Kratschmer, though, also puts better than he ever has, with his third throw reaching into the 48-feet range, and Avilov goes a foot over his own p.r. with his third throw of 14.81 meters, well over 48 feet. Dixon, with a best of 14.44 meters, is a full 4 feet under his p.r. Even though seven events remain, he is almost surely out of contention for a medal. There are too many other athletes scoring too well for him to make up enough ground.

The standings after three events:

1. Kratschmer   2,562
2. Jenner   2,493
3. Pihl   2,461
5. Avilov   2,451
11. Dixon   2,376

So far Kratschmer has seemed to be the ideal decathlete. Physically, he is imposing, with a muscular torso, maybe the only decathlete in Montreal more impressively developed than Jenner. He has cultivated a crop of blond hair that is unruffled by sprinting, jumping, or throwing. His good looks are almost a parody, like a Nordic version of a California beachboy. And with his strong shot-putting, he seems to be without an athletic flaw. But now is the high jump. Surely, if ever a body was unsuited to the demands of this event, it

167

would be Kratschmer's. His bulk seems just too great to pass over the height that he will need to stay ahead of Jenner.

Again, there are two jumping pits and two groups of jumpers. Kratschmer, Avilov, Dixon, and Jenner are all in the same group. Most of the weaker jumpers fail to clear 2.0 meters (6-6¾). Only eight are left jumping at that height.

One of those is Kratschmer. His big body is awkward, but his headfirst style is flawless. He goes over on his first try at 2 meters. So does Avilov, and so does Jenner.

The bar is moved to 2.03 meters, the height that stopped Jenner a month earlier at the Trials. Now the portable benches near the jumping area are nearly empty, with most of the athletes having left to sit on the grass infield to wait for the 400-meter run.

Kratschmer misses his first attempt at that height. Jenner misses his first jump. Avilov, incredibly, passes at the height. Kratschmer misses his second, badly. Jenner misses his second when the back of his calves brush the bar. But Kratschmer clears on his third attempt.

First Jenner must wait for Raimo Pihl's third jump. He seems not to notice when Pihl hits the bar and fails. Jenner walks to the bar after it has been replaced by two officials. He raises his left knee and both arms in a mimicry of the takeoff technique. He walks back to the scrap of adhesive tape which marks the starting point of his approach. He walks through his pattern of steps that culminate in an oblique, glancing angle toward the bar. He walks back to the tape. His face is blank, no suggestion of fear or even grimness. His lips are pressed tight together in concentration, but he does that often before a jump or a throw, even in practice. He takes a relaxed stance at the tape. He is motionless for five, ten seconds, and then he begins to run. He swerves toward the bar. Step, step, and then jump. The head and shoulders are over. The hips follow. He raises his knees just at the moment when it seems the calves will brush the bar again. His head is cocked to his left side and (a photograph will show later) his eyes are focused over his left shoulder at one end of the bar.

He plops, head and shoulders first, into the landing pad. There is a glance to be sure that the bar has held, and then he raises clenched fists over his head. He scrambles off the pad, walks to his spot on one of the benches, screws the top from the unlabeled bottle, and gulps the green liquid inside.

Both Kratschmer and Jenner miss three consecutive jumps at the next height, 2.06, so their relative position does not change. But Avilov does not miss at 2.06.

The bar goes to 2.08. Avilov is the only jumper left at this height. He misses his first jump but sails over the second time.

At 2.10, Avilov misses his first jump. Jenner, in his sweatsuit, sits on the bench and folds a towel, then stretches out on the bench, towel under his head, and watches Avilov's second jump. The Russian goes over easily.

At 2.12, Avilov ties his p.r. by clearing his second jump.

At 2.14 he misses his first try when his right leg catches the bar. He misses his second, but not so badly, when the right knee ticks the bar. He is over the third time. Two meters, 14 centimeters is equivalent to 7 feet and a quarter inch. It is also worth 975 points.

At 2.16, Avilov sends the bar flying his first two times over and finally is eliminated when his right knee again catches the bar.

Standings after four events:
1. Kratschmer 3,444
2. Avilov   3,426
3. Jenner   3,375

He had never been so happy to be in third place and trailing by 69 points.

A funny feeling started to come over me about this time. In four events so far, I'd set three personal records. My 100,

*even though I missed the p.r. there, had to be the best I
ever ran. When I cleared 6-8, I started to feel that there
was nothing I couldn't do if I had to. It was a feeling of
awesome power, except that I was in awe of myself, knock-
ing off these p.r.'s just like that. I felt that I was rising
above myself, doing things that I had no right to be doing. I
kept that feeling when we went out to run the 400. I was
hot. I wanted so much to win. I remembered that relay leg
from a couple of weeks before and I knew I could do
something like that again. I've said that it's hard to psych
out another athlete at this level of competition. There is one
way to do it. You can go out and run away from them as
you've never done before. That can do it, and that was
what I wanted to happen. I wanted to give them all something to think about overnight.*

Jenner, Kratschmer, Avilov, and Dixon all run in the same
400-meter heat at the end of the first day. Jenner draws a lane
inside Avilov and Kratschmer, with Dixon in the innermost
lane. Because of the lane stagger, Jenner will trail Avilov and
Kratschmer until his own shorter path through the turns
makes up the difference.

But even so, there is no question that he is the fastest man
on the track. By the end of the back straightaway, he has
already made up the distance. In the last turn, he is running a
shorter distance and also is running harder than anyone else.
He runs away from Dixon. He passes Avilov and he passes
Kratschmer without pause. He leads coming into the finishing straight and the lead grows larger as he comes to the thin
tape stretched across the finish line.

He barges through the tape and is still running close to full
speed when he throws his head back to look at the timer on
the scoreboard ahead and above him. It reads 47.5 seconds.

Kratschmer and Avilov cross the line almost simulta-
neously, both more than a half-second behind Jenner.

The standings after the first day:

1. Kratschmer   4,333
2. Avilov   4,315
3. Jenner   4,298

When I saw the clock, saw what I'd run, I threw my hands up. Right then, I knew I had it. I had the gold. I knew it and everybody else there on the field knew it, too, just as long as I made a mark in every event the next day and came just reasonably close to doing what I was capable of doing. I slept pretty well that night.

The sky next morning is grey and ugly. It is a day that reminds Jenner of the afternoon when Dave Roberts went off to pole-vault in the finals. This time Jenner, too, carries out five vaulting poles, balancing them over one shoulder as he walks down to the stadium.

He has drawn the fourth and last heat of the hurdles. He watches Dixon stumble over a hurdle and finish with a time of 18.11 in the first heat. He watches Avilov win the second heat in 14.2 seconds, a tenth of a second faster than he had run in Munich. He watches Kratschmer win the third heat in 14.56 seconds. But the prospect of dropping a few dozen points to the two men he is chasing seems more palatable than falling as Dixon did. He runs a steady but conservative race, finishing almost shoulder to shoulder with Ryszard Skowronek, the winner, on his immediate right. Skowronek has a time of 14.75. Jenner's clocking is 14.84.

After six events:
1. Avilov   5,254
2. Kratschmer   5,228
3. Jenner   5,164

I ran too slow. It's the only event that disappointed me. But it affected me to see Dixon fall. I'd seen it happen before. Jeff Bennett would have had a medal if he hadn't gotten hit by Katus in the hurdles in Munich. It happens.

It hurt me to see that happen to Dixon. He's such a talented athlete. Because he did poorly in the Olympics, people are liable to forget that he was one of the great decathletes. But that's the nature of the sport in this country. There's only one big meet every four years, only one meet that anybody pays any attention to. Fewer fans come out to see the national championships every year than you'll find in just about any movie house in the country on a Saturday night.

So I figured I'd drop a few points. Avilov ran the hurdles so nicely, so smoothly. I had to admire him. His first three events the first day were poor and it looked as though he was out of it. So what does he do? A new p.r. in the high jump, a new p.r. in the 400, and then a beautiful hurdles race like that. All of a sudden he's leading. I didn't figure that he would lead for long, and neither did he, I guess. But a lot of guys would have folded up right in the middle of the first day when things started going badly for him at the start.

When the race was over, I tried to forget about the hurdles. I had to put out of my mind the points I could have gotten and be thankful that I didn't fall. And it worked. I concentrated on the discus and I got back that same feeling I'd had the afternoon of the first day.

There is a white ribbon stretched in an arc across the pie-shaped chunk of the stadium infield that is used for the discus throw. The ribbon marks 50 meters from the edge of the discus-throwing circle. On his second warm-up throw, Jenner hits the ribbon. His first throw in the competition hits almost exactly the same place—50.04 meters, the scoreboard says. His second and third throws are both 49.16 meters. The third is probably the strongest throw of all. But its trajectory is lower than it should be. It hits the ground and skips long and hard.

The third throw should have gone farther. I just didn't get it up as high as I could have. It had the force and the velocity. You could tell that from the way it went flying after it hit the ground. After the first throw, I tried to really muscle the last two. I tried too hard. But I almost nailed that third one.

The throw is worth 873 points. It is the longest throw of the competition. Kratschmer has begun to show flaws for the first time. For all of his muscle, he throws the discus only 45.7 meters on his best throw. Avilov strains to get his best to 45.6 meters.

After seven events:

1. Avilov   6,046
2. Jenner   6,037
3. Kratschmer 6,019

Jenner is so much better than the others in the three remaining events that there is only one way that he can lose the gold medal. That is to fail to make a single jump in the pole vault. Such failure would seem to be an absurd notion if it had not happened before—and just a year earlier, at the AAU meet in Santa Barbara. There are a few dozen people in the stands wearing yellow *"GO JENNER GO"* T-shirts who remember that day. And they file out of the stadium with all the rest of the spectators as the stadium is cleared around noon. There are two different seatings, the first from morning until noon and the second from afternoon until evening. So the stadium is empty when the athletes walk down to the pole-vaulting pits and begin their warm-ups. Chrystie waits outside with friends and family, standing in front of the turnstiles, holding her ticket for the afternoon events and waiting for the ticket-takers to motion the crowd through the gates. She waits more than a half hour before the signal comes and she can go running back to her seat.

When she reaches the seat, she sees Jenner lying on a

bench near the vaulting runway, tossing a roll of adhesive tape into the air, catching it in his left hand, tossing it up again. He does not even glance up as the other athletes jump. The bar is at 4.40 meters—14 feet, 5¼ inches.

"Come on, Bruce," she says softly. "Make a height. Make a height and get it over with. Come on, Bruce."

She clutches a program, twists it in her hands, as the bar is raised to 4.45 meters, then to 4.50. Still Jenner lies on the bench. Finally the scoring chart for the vault flashes over the scoreboards. Jenner, it says, has already cleared his first height with a jump of 4.30 meters. He cleared his opening height while the stadium was empty. Now he is waiting for the bar to go higher before he jumps again. It is over. The gold medal is his. On their best days, neither Kratschmer nor Avilov will vault high enough, throw the javelin far enough, or run the 1500 meters fast enough to stave off Jenner.

Pretty ironic. The stadium was empty when I made that first jump. I knew I was jumping to clinch the gold. But nobody was watching except the athletes, the officials, and a few ushers. I passed the first few heights and then I told the officials that I would be jumping at 4.30 meters. I stood beneath the bar when my turn came and thought, this is ridiculous. I've worked so hard, and it comes down to this. A good warm-up height. Nothing. Nothing. It was all so different from the way I'd imagined it. I always figured the crowd would be roaring and I'd be running my butt off in the 1500 meters. But the place was totally still and I had all the time in the world to think about what I was doing. I walked over to Fred Samara. I told him, "Freddie, this is it. All I've got to do is go over the bar and I'll be the Olympic champion."

He knew what I was talking about. He sensed the way I felt, because he looked at me and he smiled and he said, "Yeah, it looks so easy."

And it was. I cleared the bar with about 2 feet to spare
and then I went back to the bench for a while, just to rest.

At 4.55 meters, Avilov misses three straight jumps and is credited with a best of 4.40. At 4.60 meters, Jenner goes chasing the world record. He vaults for the second time that afternoon. His first jump at 4.60 is high enough, but he knocks the bar away as he falls toward the cushion. Kratschmer clears on his first try at 4.60. Jenner picks up a pole, walks off to the front straight of the running track to practice his approach, then returns and easily clears the height on his second attempt. He is over with at least a foot to spare. With Avilov out of the vaulting competition, Jenner takes the overall lead with that successful jump.

At 4.70 meters, Jenner misses his first two tries. So does Kratschmer. Jenner pulls off his T-shirt—it is the one he wore at Eugene, the one that says, "FEET DON'T FAIL ME NOW" across the front—and he walks down to the vaulting pit to walk through the planting motion, jabbing the end of the pole in the plant box and then bending the pole with both arms. He walks back to the end of the runway and is ready to vault when the loudspeakers boom out the announcement of a medal ceremony and three very husky women file out to the white, wooden three-tiered stand which sits beside the front straightaway of the running track. The Olympic anthem blares. The announcement, first in French and then in English, says that this will be the awarding of medals for the women's discus throw.

The women bend down to receive the medals, Jenner pulls on his T-shirt, sips from his bottle, and waits until the music has been played and the women have left the stand and the flags have been hoisted up the three flagpoles at one end of the stadium and then brought down again.

Now he can jump. The crowd knows why he needs these points. In the back rows, the spectators rise from their chairs as he gallops down the runway. There is a clatter as the seats of the chairs, under spring tension, snap against the chair backs. Scattered shouts and squeals break the silence in the stadium and there is a collective intake of breath as he rises off the stadium floor, twists his body over the bar, seems to hang suspended, then throws the pole away and falls to the cushion without disturbing the bar. There is a lot of cheering, because there are a lot of Americans in the capacity crowd and after the first day of the decathlon they know who he is and what he is trying to do.

Kratschmer misses his third and last try at 4.70. There are three decathletes still in the vaulting area: Jenner, Skowronek, and the young Frenchman, Bobin. Jenner passes at 4.75 meters—15 feet, 7 inches. And as he picks up his pole to vault at 4.80, he has more than the jump on his mind.

I darned near got disqualified, right there in the pole vault. It was so dumb. But it almost happened.

Every vaulter uses a spray-on adhesive, a kind of stick-um, to get a good grip on his pole. It's perfectly legal. But the International Amateur Athletic Federation has a rule that you can't spray the stuff on your pole, only on your hands. The rule is never enforced, though. Everybody sprays the stuff on his pole. I have for as long as I can remember. I sprayed it on my pole when I was getting ready to jump after I'd made the opening height, and an official stopped me. He said, "Hey, you can't spray that stuff on the pole." I said fine, I wouldn't do it again. I jumped and I forgot about it.

I was jumping at 4.70 about an hour later. A pressure situation. I wasn't thinking about the stickum. I'd already missed twice and I needed the vault. Without thinking, I sprayed the stuff on the pole again. This time the official came over and said to me: "This is my last warning. Do it again and I'm going to disqualify you."

I didn't do it again.

He knocks the bar off on his first jump at 4.80. The bar, painted fluorescent orange with three black bands near the center, is cranked back up the aluminum standards to the height of 4.80 meters. Jenner poises at the end of the runway and begins his approach. Again, the clatter of the chairs. Again, the shouts and yelps and squeals. And again, Jenner is over. He falls feet-first with his arms already raised in triumph over his head. Sometime earlier, Jenner had spotted Chrystie in the crowd, and now he looks up at her and grins before he climbs off the cushion.

He has equaled his p.r. and left Kratschmer and Avilov to fight for second place. He misses his first two tries at the next height, 4.90. Instead of practicing his planting motion before the third jump, he is off to one side pretending to throw the javelin. No surprise, then, when he gets a bad lift off the ground on his third try and passes beneath the bar.

After eight events:

1. Jenner   7,042
2. Kratschmer 6,976
3. Avilov   6,966

I had a half hour before I was supposed to start throwing the javelin. I lay down in the grass and put a towel over my face. I started to cry. It was a bittersweet moment for me. I knew I was going to win the gold medal. I figured I would break the world record if I got a good javelin throw. But this was also the last decathlon of my life. With the tension and the pressure gone, the emotion started to take over. This was my life, and now it was ending. After a while I took the towel off my face and looked around at the crowd. The stadium was full of people. I tried to take it all in, all the people and the cheering. I realized that no matter what I might ever do with the rest of my life, I'd never be in this position again. This was the end of my athletic life, the last time I would ever be so involved in the Olympics. I wanted to enjoy it while I could.

177

Litvinenko got me out of that mood. He walked over to
me while I was lying there and kind of patted me on the
shoulder.
"Bruce, you going to be Olympic champion," he said.
"Thanks," I said.
Then he looked at me for a couple of seconds.
"Bruce," he said, "you going to be millionaire?"
I had to laugh.

For his first throw in the javelin, Jenner selects a heavy-tipped instrument known as a "low-meter" javelin. The imbalance makes a long throw almost impossible. But it also reduces the chance of a foul throw. He is taking no chance now. The trajectory is high. With the heavy nose, the javelin sinks almost straight into the turf. The throw measures 61.26 meters. Now he can go back to a more normal javelin. The second throw travels 68.12, and the third, 68.52 meters—224 feet, 10 inches. It pushes his total high enough that he needs only a relatively slow time of 4.35 in the 1500 meters to set a new world record.

After nine events:

1. Jenner   7,904
2. Kratschmer 7,716
3. Avilov   7,655

Avilov and I sat together while we were waiting to run the
1500 meters. He congratulated me. I traced out "7904"
with my finger on the bench. He shook his head, kind of
whistled, and said, "A lot of points, Bruce. A lot of points."
I felt sorry for him that day. I don't know that much
about him, but I know he must be a proud guy. You have to
be, to reach that level. You've got to have pride and a
pretty big ego. But he was out there, watching, while some
other guy came along and took away the gold medal and
blew his Olympic record right out of the books. He had to
sit there and watch it, knowing that there was nothing he

*could do about it. The decathlon is brutal that way. You
can't run away and hide when you run a bad race. You've
got to stand out there and suffer for two days. Which he
did, knowing that the best he could do after that first day
was a silver medal. I don't know how he felt about it, but I
know how I would have felt. If I had won the gold medal
and set an Olympic record four years before, I don't think I
could have gotten too excited about the prospect of winning
a silver medal.*

*He was right about one thing. I did have an awful lot of
points. Some very good decathletes go a long time without
ever scoring 7,900 in an entire decathlon. I did. Now I had
that many with one event still to go.*

It is the evening, just a few minutes before seven. Outside
the stadium, crowds are already gathering for a semifinal
soccer match to be held on the field in one hour. But the
stands now are still full of track and field fans. Perhaps two-
thirds of the original 70,000 are still in their seats. Many of
them are Finns, staying to watch the medal ceremony in the
5000-meter run, won earlier in the afternoon by their national hero, Lasse Viren. But most of the crowd is from the
United States. It has been a bad day for those Americans who
take their track and field laced with a heavy dose of
nationalism. They have heard the Russian national anthem
and the East German national anthem and the Cuban national anthem. But no American today has won a gold medal.
An American, James Butts, has lost to Russian Viktor Saneev
in the final round of the triple jump. Maxie Parks and Fred
Newhouse, Jenner's two relay teammates in the practice field
meet, were caught and passed by the Cuban Juantorena in
the 400 meters. Now the American fans are hanging around
for a sure thing.

The clouds are thick and grey overhead, as they have been
all day. So the big banks of lights around the roof of the
stadium are burning, and the combination of the dusky sun-

light and the tungsten glare puts the field and the athletes in a surreal, shimmering, otherworldly tone.

The 1500 meters is equivalent to 4,921 feet, or about 359 feet short of a mile. It is close enough to be known as the "metric mile," usually by Americans who cannot otherwise relate to the regularity of the metric system. A mile race consists of four laps around a 440-yard track. In the 1500 meters, the runners start at a line at the head of the backstretch, run three consecutive full laps of 400 yards each and another three-quarters of a lap, 300 meters, to finish along the front straight.

Now the athletes gather at that line of the backstretch. Jenner jogs in a full warm-up suit, ready to run the last of perhaps 10,000 miles he put behind him in six years. He stops and stands at attention for the 5000-meter medal ceremony and the Finnish anthem. When that is finished, he strips down to his uniform, jogs a few more seconds, and goes to the line. Samara, who has run in an earlier heat, walks over to him with less than a minute to go.

"Go get it," Samara says. "I want to see you do it."

Jenner has drawn the outermost lane, but that means little. In any race longer than 400 meters, runners are allowed to drop down from the high lanes to the inside of the track. That is what happens when the gun goes off. The line of runners converges on the inside lane. Litvinenko, starting in the fourth lane, near the middle of the track, rushes out to take the lead and the field strings out behind him. Avilov is second going into the turn. Jenner is behind him. Litvinenko's pace is astonishingly fast for a man competing in the final event of an Olympic decathlon. He builds his lead. Near the middle of the front straight, Jenner lopes past Avilov. Kratschmer chases Avilov. Litvinenko's lead, maybe 40 yards, grows no larger.

I went out to run the best race I could. I figured that I would run a decent pace the first 800 meters and see where

180

I stood and how I felt. I didn't want to run myself out too early, but I knew that I needed a 4:15 to get 8,600 points, and I'd be lying if I told you I didn't think about that.

In my warm-ups I felt as strong as I'd ever felt before a 1500. There's a clock beside the starting line. It starts at the gun and it's big enough and placed in such a way that the runner can tell his time at the end of each lap. It hit 1:10—70 seconds—just as I finished the first lap. The next lap it read 2 minutes, 20 seconds, which means the second lap was exactly 70 seconds, too. That's a pretty good pace, and I still felt good. So I thought I'd pick it up a little. Litvinenko was so far out there that I couldn't really tell whether I was making up any ground. But I had a feeling that I must be, because the crowd started to get louder. I knew I must be doing something.

From the start of the race, there has been a sustained and anxious hum from the crowd. For this is the decathlon, and a world record will almost surely be set in the next four and a half minutes. Those in the stands who have never seen Thorpe or Mathias will be able to say that they have watched Jenner. And the noise begins to swell as Jenner glances at the clock at the end of the first 800 meters and his stride begins to lengthen. His own perspective is poor, but the change is obvious to any seat in the stands. Jenner is running faster than Litvinenko. The gap between them is growing smaller. The race shouldn't matter. Litvinenko cannot possibly win a medal. But somehow, the chase is symbolic. It is the nature of athletes to compete when they are running on the same track, and it is typical of Jenner that the sight of a man running ahead of him should make his own legs begin to churn faster.

And the sound builds. They cross the starting line a third time. Now it is a 300-meter dash to the finishing line. The clock tells Jenner that his third lap is the fastest so far, 68 seconds, and still his legs feel strong. There is no reason now to hold anything back. He has prepared himself six years for these last 300 meters. Now he can see that Litvinenko is closer. And the sound! It is tumultuous. It cascades down from the stands and beats down on his head and shoulders. It literally shakes the ground beneath his feet. It is bigger and louder than he could have imagined during those lonely winter nights when he ran alone in the darkness. Nobody could have imagined this. He lets the noise gather up inside of him and push his legs along. It really feels that way. The louder they roar, the faster he runs. His strength seems without limit. He is not conscious of pain or even of breathing. The television coverage shows a mixture of seeming ecstasy and terror on his face as his cheeks bellow and he sucks in the air.

Litvinenko hears the noise. Running into the last turn, he looks back over one shoulder. When he sees Jenner so close, he, too, begins to run harder.

He runs just hard enough. Jenner still gains through that turn and down the finishing straight. The distance between them is perhaps 4 yards when Litvinenko breaks the tape. Except for the crowd noise, he could have heard Jenner's footsteps behind him. They are that close.

That last straight. I'll have a mental picture of that moment for the rest of my life, the crowd going bananas, me putting them down and picking them up as fast as I could and gaining on Litvinenko all the time. Twenty yards from the tape, I told myself, "Don't you dare slow down now, you so-and-so." I got a last bit of adrenaline. I leaned at the finish line.

My first thought after I crossed the line was to look up at the scoreboard clock. It said Litvinenko had run 4:11.2, and I knew I wasn't much more than a second behind, and that I had the 8,600 and the record.

Then I became aware that I had my arms raised over my head and my mouth wide open. I was yelling. Nothing in particular, just screaming. All this was going through my

This was Bruce's second attempt at 4.80 meters (15 feet 9 inches). A new world record in the Decathlon hung on this jump. (James Drake for Sports Illustrated)

The third, last and best throw of the javelin that brought him closer to the Gold Medal and a new world record. (Neil Leifer for Sports Illustrated)

A moment after crossing the finish line and realizing that finally he's won it all.
(Walter Iooss, Jr. for Sports Illustrated)

The start of the victory lap. Bruce is passing the Jenner cheering section. (Neil Leifer for Sports Illustrated)

A fan gave Bruce an American flag that he waved as he took his victory lap before a standing ovation. (Wide World Photo)

Chrystie breaks down with a release of emotion as she watches Bruce start his victory lap. (Wide World Photo)

Moments later a smiling Chrystie and Bruce pose for photographers at track side. (Neil Leifer for Sports Illustrated)

The Gold Medal has just been placed around his neck and Bruce takes a deep breath as if trying to inhale the whole moment. (James Drake for Sports Illustrated)

Bruce, Chrystie and Bertha pose outside their Montreal home the day after he won the Gold Medal. (Wide World Photo)

Bruce addresses a dinner in his honor at Newtown, Conn. Behind Bruce are former Decathlon winner Bob Mathias, Chrystie, and his father Bill. They named the High School field "Bruce Jenner Stadium" in honor of their most illustrious graduate. (Wide World Photo)

head the instant I was crossing the line. I got a flash of annoyance with myself. All my life, I'd wanted a picture of myself crossing the finish line of the 1500 meters when I won the gold medal. This was the moment, and here I was looking like a dope with my mouth wide open and my arms straight up. But it was too late then to be vain. The moment was gone and then I started trotting around the track.

Litvinenko runs up to Jenner, hugs him, kisses him on the cheek. A man climbs over the low railing in front of the stands, sprints past one grey-shirted security guard, and manages to pass off a small American flag to Jenner before he is captured and arrested. So Jenner holds the flag in his hand as he jogs a complete lap of the track. The noise is louder than ever. Some reporters will call it the loudest and most sustained ovation of the Games. Jenner is drinking it in and trotting through the last turn when he sees Chrystie at the railing. She has left her seat and tries to join him. She is pushing and weeping and trying to lift herself over a barrier of guards to go down on the track. Bruce runs to the rail, reaches out, and he pulls her past the guards and onto the track.

The noise from the crowd does not stop until Jenner disappears into a door beneath the stands.

There is a wait of perhaps fifteen minutes before the medal ceremony. Most of the crowd stays, though the last athlete has gone from the field. Then the taped Olympic theme rattles the loudspeakers and the first figure appears out of the door beside the starting line. It is Kratschmer. Though Avilov finished the 1500 meters third, Kratschmer was close enough (collapsing after he crossed the line) to hold second place overall. On the victory stand, Jenner will be flanked by Kratschmer on his right and Avilov on his left. So Kratschmer leads the procession out, with Jenner and Avilov behind him.

They cross the track, turn sharply to their left, and walk behind the victory stand. They stop. Jenner's name is an-

183

nounced first. He steps up to the highest of the three platforms and bends down to receive the medal around his neck. It is heavy and shiny, and it hangs from a gold link chain. In fact, the medallion is not truly gold at all, but an alloy known as silver-gilt. The second- and third-place medals actually are silver and bronze. None of this diminishes the respect with which Jenner later drapes his medal into its walnut carrying case.

When I walked off the field after the medal ceremony, I glanced around one more time and then walked away. That was the end of the decathlon for me. I never even went back and got my vaulting poles. I left them there in the stadium. They're a hassle to travel with and I was finished with them.

It was the end of one of the most competitive episodes in decathlon history. Not only Jenner, but also Dixon and Avilov, had announced before the Games that this would be their last meet.

Aftermath

There was a party that night in the dining room of a motel near the stadium, the motel where Chrystie had stayed. If the celebration at Eugene had been like a graduation party, this was more on the order of a small wedding reception. There was champagne, more champagne, a lot of raucous laughter, and a few tears. There were also some microphones and cameras and floodlights, but for a long time there were no Bruce and Chrystie. They were the last to arrive—there had been a sudden command performance in the ABC studios —and they finally walked arm in arm into the banquet room about an hour before midnight, with the medal swinging from its chain around Chrystie's neck. Somebody caught the glint of the gold medal in one of the TV floodlights and people began to shout and yell and laugh. Bruce held a magnum of champagne in his hands, took a long pull, took another long pull for a film cameraman who hadn't been able to muscle in for a shot the first time. The medal was passed around for inspection. There were jokes about Graceland College and toasts to working wives and the whole affair went on much longer than it had any right to, because this was a rare moment of pure joy and abandonment. Fatigue and impatient looks from the management finally intervened. Bruce

187

and Chrystie were not the first to leave, but neither were they the last. No motel tonight, and no crowded apartment in the Village. Someone had found a room at the Queen Elizabeth Hotel. The manager of the banquet room presented Chrystie with a bill as she was leaving. She had asked to buy a dozen bottles of champagne. The bill was for 50 bottles. She began to complain.

Bruce reached for the check and shoved it into his pocket. He would pay it, he told the manager. He leaned close to his wife as they left the room.

"It doesn't matter," he said. "Not tonight. Not any more."

The next day Jenner was at a cocktail party and was introduced to Michael O'Hara, president of the International Track Association, the major organizer and promoter of professional track meets. O'Hara suggested that Jenner might want to consider an offer to compete with the ITA, since his decision to retire from amateur competition had been known in the track community for several months.

> *I tried to be polite. The truth was that I didn't think they could afford me. But the way I put it was that I expected that I would have a lot of offers to do things outside athletics. If I were going to compete in athletics, I said, then I would want to devote a lot of time to training, which would detract from all these other things. But I told him to talk to my new manager, George Wallach.*

Among the rules governing an amateur athlete is that he enter into no contract with a business manager. George Wallach, head of a Beverly Hills firm which specializes in radio and TV time sales, had met the Jenners in 1975. They became friends and he began to act as a personal advisor and a buffer against some of the more aggressive demands for Jenner's time and energy, all within the letter of the amateur code and all without compensation. On July 31, 1976, he

188

became personal manager for both the Jenners, Chrystie by now having become a familiar face through the ABC coverage as well as features and interviews by other networks and national magazines.

First, though, Jenner had his joke. He strode up to Wallach at the celebration the night of the 30th. "Wallach," he said, "your percentage just went down. I made it too easy for you." Wallach did not smile for the first few seconds.

The next day, I was talking to George and I found out that O'Hara offered a four-year contract at $50,000 a year. George turned it down. That shook me up for a minute. Somebody is offering me $200,000 for doing something I've been doing for nothing all my life. And we turn it down.

There was an offer that same Saturday morning from a men's toiletry company: $50,000 for a single one-minute commercial spot. Wallach turned that down, too. He was more interested, he said, in a long-term arrangement, and a figure with five zeroes at the end.

That Saturday Jenner went into a pizza parlor in downtown Montreal. He spent much of the time shaking hands and signing autographs. He was visible. He was known. People pointed at him. But his life was still relatively placid until three days later, when his parents drove him and Chrystie out of Montreal, across the border. The first stop was his parents' home. There was a banner strung across the street near the house and a crowd that included a few neighbors and a lot of strangers.

That was to be expected. This was a local kid made good. But that afternoon they flew into New York City and it was the same. When they walked down Fifth Avenue, people yelled from cars and from across the street. One man stopped his car in the middle of rush hour traffic, jumped outside, and began to shout, waving his hands above his head.

They had a suite at the Sherry Netherland Hotel. The

suite, Chrystie noted, was larger than their apartment in San Jose. They were to appear the next morning on a network talk show, and they rode to the studio in a black limousine that had been furnished by the network.

(Before they could be paid the standard appearance fee, Bruce had to fill out a W-2 Internal Revenue Service form for tax purposes. He hadn't seen such a thing in years. This was, in fact, the first money he had earned since getting a leave of absence from the insurance company more than six months earlier.)

That morning there was a press conference in the offices of the Jenners' new public relations firm. Forty print media outlets were invited. Sixty arrived, plus cameramen from the major TV stations and reporters from most of the important radio stations. That afternoon their photographs appeared in the New York *Post*. There would be a half dozen photographs in the *Daily News* the next morning, taken as they strolled down Fifth Avenue, bought a pretzel from a vendor, chatted with passersby.

They ate dinner that night at a popular East Side restaurant and turned away bottles of champagne sent by diners. For a day, at least, the city was his. He watched a rehashing of the Games on television that night, the first time he had seen any of the ABC coverage. He spoke on the phone to an acquaintance in California as he sat beside a window and watched traffic on Park Avenue sliding silently below.

"I'm riding the wind," he said.

He was taking it all with unabashed delight. He would take it as long as it lasted.

He and Chrystie returned to California long enough to pack their bags again and fly to the island of Hawaii. They had visited Oahu twice before. Using her flying privileges with the airline and eating take-out hamburgers, they had gone to Honolulu on their honeymoon and kept a budget under $200. This trip should have cost considerably more, but they met a lot of indulgent hotel managers and restaurant owners.

None of these seemed obligatory courtesies. Bruce and Chrystie were discovering that they were somehow favorably regarded by people whom they had never met. People liked the Jenners. They were going to make a lot of money, no secret about that. (The morning after Jenner had won the gold, one of the Montreal papers, a French daily, called him "*dieu du stade*"—literally, "god of the stadium"—and also called him an instant millionaire.) But there seemed to be little resentment of his good fortune.

The TV camera had not merely made him an instant personality. It had also faithfully recorded the essential naïveté and amiability in his demeanor and his outlook. When he jumped 6-8, when he vaulted 15-9, and when he won the gold medal, he was happy and not afraid to show it. To accept such triumphs stoically and without emotion might have been more stylish, but it was not Jenner's way. He was happy, so he laughed. He seemed grateful for success. And the people liked that. They also liked his good looks and his dog and the fact that he loved his wife and said so to anyone. He was an old-fashioned hero, without pretensions or affectations, neither boastful nor coyly modest. And the country may have been ready for such a hero.

Not until you get into that sort of situation do you realize what an impact the big tube has in this country. You consider all the millions of people who saw me perform or who saw Chrystie, saw an interview. All those people, they feel as though they know us. And they do, in a lot of ways, because I've never tried to be anything but myself in that situation. A lot of them were sitting in front of the TV on that Friday night and yelling and screaming just as hard as my own parents. They feel a part of what I've done, and in a sense they are, too. But it's not just in one town or one city. It's everywhere, everywhere people have a TV set, and there are so many of them out there that I don't think anybody can comprehend the numbers.

We went to Hawaii trying to get away. Not that the people were bothering us. It's just that it seemed so far away from Montreal and all that had gone on there. We were out on a fishing boat in the middle of the ocean when another boat came alongside, about 40 yards away. I saw a woman on the boat. She looked, she looked again, and then she started waving and yelling.

"It's you," she said, over and over again. "It's you, it's really Bruce Jenner."

After a while, I guess, people in the public eye get used to that kind of thing happening. And maybe I'll get blasé about it after a while. But right now, I really can't get over it.

The impact was not limited to strangers. When Chrystie's mother visited them after they returned from Montreal, she came through the front door with some reluctance.

"She felt terrible," Chrystie says. "I asked her what was wrong and she wouldn't talk for a minute, and finally she blurted out that she was afraid we had changed, that we looked so far away and unapproachable on TV. Bruce and my father have enjoyed playing golf, whenever Bruce had the time. Now she said she was afraid that Bruce wouldn't want to play golf with my dad. She kept saying, 'I want to hold Bruce, I just want to hold him.' Bruce was on the phone but he gave her a big hug. That made her feel better. But it made me realize what television can do."

In the ten weeks after he won the gold medal, Bruce Jenner:

• appeared as a guest on four national television interview or variety programs;

• teamed with Rafer Johnson to lose a doubles tennis match to Ethel Kennedy and Jean Smith, also on national television;

• spent four days with his father in a Louisiana swampland, working with an alligator relocation crew during the

192

filming of an episode of "The American Sportsman," another network TV show;

- attended a state dinner at the White House, and was seated beside Betty Ford;
- was the guest of honor at a ceremony in his old home town to rename the football field at Newtown High School, with the new plaque reading: "Bruce Jenner Stadium";
- established a p.r. in a new category by signing 600 autographs during a 2¼-hour appearance at a store opening in Pennsylvania;
- flew to Rome to test for the Superman role;
- signed a two-year contract for an undisclosed sum to serve as a sports commentator and an actor with the ABC network; and
- played golf for two days with Chrystie's father in the Crownovers' annual family outing.

They finally rested and spent five days at home in San Jose early in October. It was about that time that Chrystie said:

"I seem to miss the decathlon more than he does. He's caught up in other things. I didn't realize how tough it would be on me to put the decathlon out of our life. It's been such a big part of our existence ever since we've known each other.

"When Bruce was in the hotel studying his lines for the screen tests, he pulled a chair out of the corner of the room and pretended it was a hurdle, just the way he always did before a meet when he wanted to work on his technique. This time he was just reaching back for something familiar in this situation that was so new to him. But when I saw it, I started to cry. I missed the decathlon. I couldn't help it."

The Record

Nearly lost in the flush of Jenner's gold medal triumph was the act which brought him that victory. It was the finest decathlon of his career and also one of the more remarkable track and field performances of recent years. Track fans dote on statistics and even make a point of distinction between world records. There are, they claim, "hard" records and "soft" records. A soft record, they say, is in jeopardy every time world-class athletes gather to contest the particular event; it seems overdue to fall. A hard record is less approachable. It is a mark regarded as beyond the reasonable efforts of any active competitor. The classic is Bob Beamon's record long jump of 29 feet, 2½ inches, set in the 1968 Games in Mexico City. The record is almost nine years old and nobody has yet come close to it. By the end of the 1976 track season, no other athlete had long-jumped as far as even 28 feet. Progress in that event is measured in fractions of inches, and it is possible that the athlete who will one day surpass it is as yet unborn.

Bruce Jenner's 8,618 is not so untouchable. Any speculation about the longevity of the record ought to be tempered by the knowledge that Avilov's 1972 world record was considered far ahead of its time and safe from assault. The possibility exists that somebody, somewhere, will exceed the record early in the 1977 track season. But decathlon expert Frank Zarnowski doubts that will happen, and he is not alone.

"It's a long way out there," Zarnowski said after the Games in Montreal. "It's so far out that nobody else in the world but Jenner could seriously think of going out and scoring that many points right now. That's the first step in setting a world record. It doesn't just happen. Somebody with a lot of ability has to be convinced that he's ready to do it. Another thing in Bruce's favor is that hand-timed records probably won't be accepted from now on. If a mark isn't electronically timed, I doubt that the IAAF will consider it. That puts about a 90-point burden on anybody who goes after the mark. The fact that Bruce's record was electronically timed makes it that much more formidable and impressive."

Taking into account the estimated two-tenths second advantage in hand-timing, Zarnowski calculates that Jenner's Montreal decathlon, if timed by stopwatch, would have exceeded 8,700 points.

Even at 8,618, Jenner was 164 points better than Avilov's figure, the previous electronic record. That is an increase of almost 2 percent, which seems negligible until one considers that a 2 percent increase in the pole vault would raise the record in that event by an improbable 4¼ inches. Two percent of the world record in the 100-meter dash is an equally improbable two-tenths of a second. In the mile run, lowering the record by 2 percent would bring it down by 4.5 seconds.

There is still another perspective on Jenner's Montreal performance. He became the only decathlete ever to score 8,600 under the present tables. He was already the only man ever to go over 8,500 on the tables. Only Avilov, Bill Toomey, Kratschmer, and Jenner ever scored more than 8,400 points; of those four, only Kratschmer was still competing after the 1976 Games, and there were rumors that he, too, had tired of the rigorous training demands. Besides Kratschmer, there are only two active decathletes who have ever broken 8,300 points: the Russian, Grebeniuk, and Zeilbauer, an Austrian. At Montreal they were far outclassed by Jenner.

It could stand for a while. It could also fall at any time. Some guy could come out of nowhere the way I did and break it any time. Back in 1972, when Avilov set his record, there was no way anybody could have seen me improving enough to break it. But I did.

At the moment, though, I'd guess that it will be around for a while. It's big enough that it has to scare anybody who takes a look at it. Even Kratschmer. The guy had the decathlon of his life at Montreal. He was 30 points over his old p.r. and about 200 points over his 1975 p.r. And even so, he finished more than 200 points behind me. That has to make him wonder.

My feeling is that as long as the record stands, fine, I'm happy. It's a great honor. But it won't last forever. Some young guy will come along and he won't be one bit impressed. He'll look at it and say, "Hey, that's not so bad. I can do that." And he will. Maybe it'll be tomorrow. Maybe ten years. When it happens, I'll send the guy a congratulatory telegram. I know what it's like to have somebody else's record out there in front of you and to give your life away to chasing it.

The day after the Games, I asked Jenner whether this decathlon was his limit, the best that he might expect to do. I asked him the question two months later and his answer was the same. As usual when he talked about the decathlon, he danced on the narrow edge of outrageous egotism. And, as usual, he managed to keep his balance.

There's no reason why I couldn't improve if I stayed with it. From 1974 to 1975, I increased my p.r. by 200 points. From my world record in 1975 to the world record in the Games a year later is almost another 100—more, if you

199

count the difference between electronic and hand-timing. I'm still at my peak and probably will be for the next two or three years. If I kept on working just as hard, I'd have to keep improving. I don't think a hand-timed 8,900 would have been out of the question within a couple of years. In fact, it's not impossible to gain 300 points from one year to the next, given enough effort on the training field. Thirty points an event isn't so tough. That's a little more than a tenth of a second in the 100, 6 inches in the long jump, five seconds in the 1500. You'd have to be lucky, put it all together in one meet, and you'd also have to be very lucky with your health. But it could be done.

The main problem is incentive, and I don't have it. Not any more. I can't believe that winning another gold medal or putting the world record farther out of reach can mean as much to me as this one did. I really marvel at a guy like Willie Davenport, the hurdler. He'd already been in the Olympics three times before, he already had a gold medal, and he was coming back from a really serious knee operation just a year before, yet he still qualified for the Olympic team this year and ended up with a bronze medal. And he seemed just like a kid in his first Olympics, just as enthusiastic.

I couldn't do it. Yesterday I drove by the track at San Jose State, where I did a lot of training. I looked out the window at the rest of those guys and I felt sorry for them. And right then, I knew I'd made the right decision to quit when I did.

"There has to be
a better way"

A Proposal

*I was lucky. I don't mean in the competition, but in the fact
that I had a wife who made decent money and who was just
as committed to seeing me win the gold medal as I was. In
this country, unless an amateur athlete has a working wife
or a wealthy family or a very tolerant boss, the odds are
that he's never even going to get a chance to try for a gold
medal. The notion of devoting your whole life to training
for a single goal is very romantic, but the realities of life are
something else again. You have to eat and pay rent and buy
equipment and you don't do that by running amateur
track. The greatest desire is no match for the bill collector.
Bills will win out over dreams every time and, as a result,
this country is wasting an incredible pool of athletic talent,
the kind of talent the Russians and the East Germans can't
even hope for. Our successes—including my own—
shouldn't be used as a defense of the system, because the
system is inefficient and, in many cases, degrading to
the athlete. I know world-record holders in this country
who couldn't buy groceries if not for food stamps.*

There has to be a better way.

*Up to a point, our system is the best in the world. Our
coaches are the best. They're innovators. Most of what the*

rest of the world knows about training and technique comes from us. And there isn't a better way of developing young athletes than the junior high–high school–junior college–university system we have here. The athletes with the talent and the incentive are the ones who succeed and earn the scholarships. The coaches are good and you can see thousands of great young athletes getting better and better, right through college. Then comes graduation day. And then comes the bombshell. No more dormitories. No more scholarships. No more coaching. The athlete is out there in the cold, cruel world with nobody but himself, and he's supposed to keep up a track career and begin to make a living at the same time. Most of them can't do it. Some of them do, somehow. It's a tribute to their own ingenuity and talent. That's the only reason we've done as well as we have in international meets and the Olympic Games so far.

This shortcoming isn't so serious in swimming, where the athletes develop so much younger. In college they're at their peak. They're getting the coaching when they need it most. But in track and field, an athlete is just beginning to realize his potential at age 21 or 22. The next few seasons are still crucial to him, but he's got nothing except what he can provide for himself.

Finances are just part of the problem. We're also far behind the East Europeans in the field of sports medicine. They have a big advantage there, and it's a subject that is becoming more and more important every year.

I'll use anabolic steroids as an example. They're illegal under Olympic rules. But the Russians and the East Germans use them to develop the muscles on their shot-putters and discus throwers, and our athletes have to use them too if they are even going to stay in the same ballpark. It's no secret. But the East Germans have doctors who know these drugs and know the tests and know when and how to use them so that you can still pass the urinalysis at the Village. Not our athletes. They have to take their own chances, hit and miss. Most of what we know about sports medicine comes to us from word of mouth when a U.S. athlete starts a conversation with a German or a Russian. That's how we learn.

I'd say that we're at a crossroads now. We're at a point where, if nothing is done very soon, we're due for a lot of embarrassment in the Olympics. It's already too late to get any long-range benefit from a program in time for the 1980 Games. But we still have time to help some of the athletes who ought to be representing us then. It's a matter of how important we choose to make athletics and the Games. Other nations approach track and field as a test of their own social and political systems. When an East German athlete beats an American, he's not just a gold medal winner. He's a war hero. The next Olympic Games will be in Moscow in 1980. This is the Russians' big chance to showcase all the products of their sports programs before their own people, and to humiliate us in the process. I know how they approach these things and I know, I just know, that they are putting together a collection of athletes that will make us look foolish in 1980 if we don't do something fast.

Some people have talked about tax subsidies for athletes or a program for corporations to hire athletes and then allow them a certain number of training days a year. I think that's a good idea, but it doesn't go far enough. It still doesn't touch the problems of administration and systematic training.

When I was an athlete, I never complained a great deal about the people who run amateur sports in this country. For one thing, that's not my style. I'll generally put up with a problem rather than hassle it out with other people. I'm a softie. And unless the problem directly affected me, I tended to ignore it. That's wrong, maybe, but I'm not an activist. It's not my nature.

But I'll say it now. The organizations that run amateur

sports in this country beyond the collegiate level, the Amateur Athletic Union and the U.S. Olympic Committee, need to be changed or replaced. The athletes and the financial contributors get too little return from what they put into the organizations. After so many years dealing with the administrators, I can't escape the conclusion that too many people in the AAU and the Olympic Committee are in it for their own benefit, egotistical if not financial. They're authoritarian beyond a reasonable point. Their decisions are too often based on politics instead of common sense. The athlete gets the impression that he is the least consequential part of the whole organization. That's how shabby the treatment is. We know that a lot of people give a lot of money to the AAU and to the Olympic Fund, but only a tiny percentage filters down to our level. As far as an attitude toward their jobs is concerned, the athletes are professionals and the administrators are amateurs.

Sometimes it's just little things, like uniforms. When I went to Russia to compete in 1974, I never got a uniform. I had to go to a Russian seamstress to have one made. That same meet, we were going to send over six decathletes while the Russians and the West Germans had nine or ten apiece. That put a lot of pressure on the Americans, since everybody had to do well in every event if we were going to have a chance of winning. Finally I made a deal with the AAU. I agreed to fly on my wife's airline pass if they would send over a seventh athlete.

I've said there ought to be a better way, and I think it has to come from the big companies and corporations in this country. It won't be cheap, but if amateur athletes in the United States are going to be running to represent the capitalist system, then the price shouldn't be too great. And it's only fitting that the money come from private areas, not the government.

My proposal is for corporations to sponsor national

training centers in the major amateur sports—especially in track and field, where it's so necessary for the athlete to have good coaching and the proper facilities after he leaves college. I'm talking about a complex with dormitories, gyms, medical facilities and all the training space and apparatus that an athlete could need. It would have to be pretty exclusive, limited to athletes who had already made the current Olympic qualifying standard in their event. The athletes who wanted to live there and train there would have all that. Personally, I wouldn't want to do it that way. So if an athlete wanted to live and train at home but work on his shot put, for example, over the winter, then he ought to be able to do that. The athletes could come and go as they wanted and needed. In this way we would have the advantages of the East European system of organized centers without the regimentation and the loss of individuality. Besides having the immediate benefit of better, stronger athletes, we would learn lessons in training, technique, and medicine that could be applied even at the junior high level. The corporations putting up the money could get all the promotional benefit they wanted from the sponsorship. The Games are already commercialized and I don't see anything wrong with that. It gets back to life's realities.

To get the maximum benefit out of this, we need a single ruling body for amateur sport. I've already griped about the AAU and the Olympic Committee. The fact that they're fragmented and sometimes fighting with the college associations for influence over athletes only makes matters worse. I don't really care who does the job of organizing and overseeing amateur sports, but the new organization ought to be a lot more streamlined and responsive to the athletes than the present ones. Most of all, it has to be free of politics.

Since I've already dwelled on what we have to look

forward to if we don't reorganize, I ought to mention what can happen if all of this comes true in the next couple of years. And that is, there is no limit to the successes possible for American athletes the day we start doing things right. There is nothing we cannot do.

Appendix

A. Great decathlons by great decathletes. Each decathlon shown represented a world record at the time, though the list is not complete. The first Total shown is from the scoring tables in use at the time. The 1962 figure, for purposes of comparison, is the corresponding total from the tables in use during Bruce Jenner's career.

	THORPE	*MORRIS*	*MATHIAS*
	Stockholm	*Berlin*	*Helsinki*
	1912	*1936*	*1952*
100-meter	11.2	11.1	10.9
Long jump	22-3¼	22-10½	22-10
Shot put	42-3½	46-3¼	50-2½
High jump	6-1⅝	6-0¾	6-2⅞
400-meter	52.2	49.4	50.2
High hurdles	15.6	14.9	14.7
Discus	121-4	141-1	153-10
Pole vault	10-8	11-6	13-1½
Javelin	149-11	178-10	194-3
1500-meter	4:40.1	4:33.2	4:50.8
Total	8,412	7,900	7,887
(1962)	6,756	7,421	7,731

Times computed electronically

JOHNSON	TOOMEY	AVILOV*	JENNER*
Eugene	Los Angeles	Munich	Montreal
1960	1969	1972	1976
10.6	10.3	11.09	10.94
24-9¼	25-5½	25-2½	23-8¼
52-0	47-2¼	47-1½	50-4¼
5-10⅛	6-4	6-11½	6-8
48.6	47.1	48.5	47.5
14.5	14.3	14.31	14.84
170-6½	152-6¼	154-1½	164-1
13-0¼	14-0½	14-11¼	15-9
233-3	215-8	202-3½	224-10
5:09.9	4:39.4	4:22.8	4:12.3
8,683	8,417	8,524	8,618
8,063	8,417	8,454	8,618

B. ABBREVIATED SCORING TABLES

100-meter
Secs. Points

100-meter		Long Jump		
Secs.	Points	Feet	Meters	Points
10.0	1072	26-0	7.91	1001
10.2	1014	25-6	7.77	974
10.4	959	25-0	7.62	945
10.6	905	24-6	7.47	915
10.8	853	24-0	7.31	884
11.0	804	23-6	7.16	853
11.2	756	23-0	7.01	822
11.5	687	22-6	6.86	791
12.0	580	22-0	6.71	758

Shot Put			High Jump		
Feet	Meters	Points	Feet	Meters	Points
53-0	16.16	856	7-3	2.20	1025
52-0	15.85	839	7-0	2.13	966
51-0	15.54	820	6-10	2.08	925
50-0	15.24	803	6-8	2.03	882
49-0	14.93	784	6-6	1.98	840
48-0	14.63	766	6-4	1.93	796
47-0	14.32	747	6-2	1.88	751
46-0	14.02	729	6-0	1.83	707
45-0	13.72	710	5-10	1.77	652

400-meter		High Hurdles		Discus		
Secs.	Points	Secs.	Points	Feet	Meters	Points
53.0	679	16.0	749	180	54.86	956
52.0	720	15.5	797	175	53.34	930
51.0	762	15.0	848	170	51.82	904
50.0	805	14.8	870	165	50.29	877
49.0	852	14.6	892	160	48.78	850
48.8	861	14.4	915	155	47.26	820
48.5	875	14.2	939	150	45.72	795
48.2	889	14.0	963	145	44.18	766
48.0	898	13.5	1023	140	42.66	737
47.8	908			135	41.14	708
47.5	923			130	39.62	678
47.2	938					
47.0	948					
46.5	973					
46.0	1000					

Pole Vault			Javelin		
Feet	Meters	Points	Feet	Meters	Points
16-5	5.00	1052	250	76.22	948
16-0	4.87	1021	240	73.16	915
15-9	4.80	1005	230	70.12	880
15-6	4.72	986	225	68.58	863
15-3	4.65	969	220	67.03	845
15-0	4.57	950	215	65.54	828
14-9	4.49	930	210	64.02	810
14-6	4.42	913	205	62.50	792
14-3	4.34	894	200	60.96	773
14-0	4.26	874	190	57.88	735
13-6	4.42	913			
13-0	3.96	796			

1500-meter

Minutes	Points
3:50	905
4:00	816
4:05	775
4:10	735
4:15	696
4:20	660
4:25	624
4:30	590